THE LIFE OF THINGS,
THE LOVE OF THINGS

FORDHAM UNIVERSITY PRESS   NEW YORK 2015

COMMONALITIES

Timothy C. Campbell, series editor

THE LIFE OF THINGS, THE LOVE OF THINGS

REMO BODEI

Translated by Murtha Baca

This book was originally published in Italian as Remo Bodei, *La vita delle cose*, Copyright © 2009, Gius. Laterza & Figli, All rights reserved. Published by arrangement with Marco Vigevani Agenzia Letteraria.

The translation of this work has been funded by SEPS
Segretariato Europeo per le Pubblicazioni Scientifiche

Via Val d'Aposa 7 - 40123 Bologna - Italy
seps@seps.it - www.seps.it

Library of Congress Cataloging-in-Publication Data available online at catalog.loc.gov.

Printed in the United States of America
17 16 15   5 4 3 2 1
First edition

CONTENTS

THE LIFE OF THINGS,
THE LOVE OF THINGS

1

OBJECTS AND THINGS

Prelude: Almost a Fantasy

With a salutary distancing effect, I shall begin by presenting several texts of a literary nature, deliberately chosen from the remote past. These texts will help us understand the genesis of our habitual relationships with things by reviving our memory of the sensation that we experience every time that, as we are waking up, we perceive the objects around us in an as yet unfocused way. At that moment, the things we see, deprived of their usual attributes, reveal themselves to be susceptible to being clothed in those multiple layers of meaning, layers of which they will subsequently be stripped once they are again treated as known entities or simply as items that can be used and exchanged.

My first literary reference is to a brief poem from the first century CE, long attributed to Virgil; the poem effectively conveys the atmosphere of things that appear in their initial indeterminacy, as they reenter the scene of the daily spectacle produced by the emanation of light, which removes them from their nocturnal hiding place and restores them to us.

The poem is called *Moretum*[1]—the Latin word for a concoction of herbs, olive oil, and cheese that is spread on bread. In it, a poor peasant, Simulus, awakening in the dark, "slowly uplifts his limbs, from the poor bed on which he had laid them, and with cautious hand he feels his way through the lifeless night, and gropes for the hearth," to revive the embers by blowing away the ashes. After he has uncovered the coals and lit the oil lamp, Simulus goes on to a tactile experience; he doesn't need light to recognize the things that he uses, once he brings them into his field of vision, to prepare his frugal morning meal, which gives the poem its title.

After the interlude of sleep, practical life takes over again and resumes its rhythms—for Simulus, the daily struggle against hunger and poverty begins anew. In the milky glow of dawn, the house and garden again take on their usual appearance. Now the light "lists" the things in the garden, distinguishing the various crops growing there: "Here flourished cabbage, here beets, their arms far outspread . . . here the roots of spiky asparagus which grow into spearpoints, and the heavy gourd, that swells into its broad belly."

A sense of wonder is reborn with the rising of the sun, at its glorious reappearance, at the gradual transition from the darkness of night to the radiance of the light of day, which reveals and paints the world in the multiplicity of its forms and colors. When the last stars fade away and the phantasms of dreams disappear, the determinacy of the day unravels the mystery of what the night had concealed.

If during the night the stars had shone, throbbing in the darkness—"*in obscura nocte sidera micant*" ("stars twinkle in the darkness of night") is written on a doorjamb at the Benedictine monastery at Subiaco in the province of Rome—now they have disappeared, and the sleeper passes from the fading away of the habitual solidity of the world to its recomposition in a familiar, solid arrangement, moving from the hallucinatory logic of desire to the pervasiveness of the harsh principle of reality. For every human being, the unfolding of intimate fears, hopes, and fantasies (which, as if in a second life, are released by sleep in the form of stories parallel to those of our waking hours) gives way to the all-consuming uniqueness of waking consciousness.

Sleep is an absolutely common and an absolutely overwhelming phenomenon that never ceases to leave us perplexed, to the point that we let ourselves suppose that some strange power has transferred us to another dimension. As if attracted by a special force of gravity, we are cyclically brought back from another space and time to return to the order and continuity of daily life; after losing ourselves in sleep, we find ourselves again. Proust used an image reminiscent of toy soldiers to describe this process of rejoining with ourselves after we return from the world of sleep:

> That kind of sleep is called "sleeping like lead," and it seems as though one has become, oneself, and remains for a few moments after such a sleep is ended, simply a leaden image. One is no longer a person. How then, seeking for one's mind, one's personality, as one seeks for a thing that is lost, does one recover one's own self rather than any other? Why, when one begins again to think, is it not another personality than yesterday's that is incarnate in one?[2]

After the parenthesis of night, everything gradually returns to its usual position in space and goes back to its predisposed compartment in our mind. The order of words and of things is reborn: we enter again into our daily routine, reconnecting with our earlier experiences and reawakening dormant anxieties, as the objects around us regain their apparent impassivity.

The ability to witness every day the night sky becoming light again, at the moment when most living things emerge from the torpor of their withdrawal into themselves, and to reconnect with the world, is a significant event for us. In predominantly agricultural, preindustrial societies—when the night had not yet been colonized by pervasive electric light, by night shifts in factories, or by nighttime revels—people generally awoke to the song of the "winged sentinel" of the morning.

The classics of literature again help us reconstruct the atmosphere that surrounded the millennial experience of innumerable individuals as they experienced the transition from dark to light, after their daily resurrection from the little death of sleep. Let us start by listening to how Virgil and Ovid describe the repose of all living beings when nature sleeps.

> Soon fell the night, and peaceful slumbers breathed
> on all earth's weary creatures; the loud seas
> and babbling forests entered on repose;
> now midway in their heavenly course the stars
> wheeled silent on; the outspread lands below
> lay voiceless; all the birds of tinted wing,
> and flocks that haunt the merge of waters wide
> or keep the thorny wold, oblivious lay
> beneath the night so still; the strings of care
> ceased troubling, and no heart its burden knew.[3]

Ovid takes up this *topos* in these verses:

> Deep slumber has relaxed the world, and all that's living, animals and birds and men, and even the hedges and the breathing leaves are still—and motionless the laden air. Only the stars are twinkling . . .[4]

Much later, in the poetry of the Austrian writer Nikolaus Lenau (set to music by Mendelssohn in his *Lieder* "*Schilflied*," opus 71, number 4), the motif returns with a reference to the birds that flutter in their sleep, immersed in the depths of a thicket of reeds in a still pond illuminated by the moon.

For an evocation of the moment of awakening in premodern societies, an intense passage from Hermann Broch's *The Death of Virgil* should suffice. Here the imminent arrival of day is announced by the traditional sound of things from the past—by the breathing of animals and the occupations and preoccupations of men heading for the marketplace:

> . . . the peasant-carts . . . traveling along in ever-narrowing rows bringing victuals to the morning market; sleepy-slow they moved onward, with a rumbling of wheels in the pavement ruts, the creaking of axles, the gritty stroke of the wheel-rims on the curbstones, the click of chains and of harnesses, sometimes with the snorting groan of an ox, sometimes with the sound of a sleepy call. . . . Breathing creatures wandered through the breath of the night, fields and gardens and nourishment wandered with them, they too breathing, and the breath of all life was opened to receive the creature . . .[5]

Orienting Oneself in the World

The last literary text that I will use to introduce issues that will be shown to have the greatest theoretical weight is better known than the texts cited above. It comes from the first pages of Proust's *Remembrance of Things Past*, when the protagonist, waking suddenly in the middle of the night, experiences a feeling of complete disorientation: he does not remember where he is, and he is almost unable to reconstruct the unity and awareness of his own self. He attempts to situate himself in space and time, to remember the positions of the furniture and walls of his room, so that "the invisible walls, changing their position according to the shape of the imagined room," will prepare the way for him to recognize the place where he is, which when he awoke seemed confused and cut off from the fluctuating outlines of the places in his memory. This sense of disorientation is fleeting; soon the narrator's awakened consciousness regains control of the situation, and his thoughts and habits restore him to his place in space and time.

But as a barely perceptible trace there remains the suspicion in the narrator's mind, aroused by the lack of immediacy in reconstructing where he is in space and time, that the presumed fixity of things is not spontaneous but rather that it essentially reflects our own rigid mental organization:

> Perhaps the immobility of the things that surround us is forced upon them by our conviction that they are themselves, and not anything else, and by the immobility of our conceptions of them.[6]

For educational purposes, in order to identify things, we disincarnate them; we condense their multiple meanings in order to classify them. By isolating things from their context and from our own sphere of activity, by conceptualizing them in our minds, we have eliminated any reference to ourselves, reducing things to material entities that simply appear before us according to an elementary, predefined typology.

> Words present to us little pictures of things, lucid and normal, like the pictures that are hung on the walls of schoolrooms to give children an illustration of what is meant by a carpenter's bench, a bird, an ant-hill, things chosen as typical of everything else of the same sort.[7]

As we grow up, we learn the names of things; we fix them in our memory, we recognize them, we highlight them against a blurry background. It is only the familiarity achieved though these processes that enables us to orient ourselves and give things a meaning. It is in this way that we learn to situate things on a spatial and temporal map, to use them or reject them, to buy or sell them, to love, hate, or be indifferent to them. In carrying out all these operations, we lose sight of the fact that our perception already reveals innumerable differences and nuances in things. The description of a simple sheet of paper lying on a table could, for example, go on forever:

> The more we look at it, the more it reveals to us its characteristics. Each new orientation of my attention, of my analysis, reveals to me a new detail: the upper edge of the sheet is slightly warped, the end of the third line is dotted . . .[8]

Because of cultural constructs and personal interests, we tend to examine carefully things that have sense and interest for us; we remove things from the inexhaustible canvas that forms the background of our field of perception, and we circumscribe them with forms suggested by the names for them in our language, by the notions we have acquired, and by our own personal projections. There is an anecdote that circulates among anthropologists about a man from a primitive civilization who is brought to a big city. He doesn't notice the buildings, trams, and automobiles, but only a bunch of bananas in a wheelbarrow, because that is the only thing that fits coherently in the framework of his experience.

Taking into account the fact that all objects are disposed to be perceived by us, tracing the outlines of things often means—at the outset—making choices: "the line does not imitate what we see—rather, it 'makes us see,'" says Klee.[9] In fact, in different cultures, the attribution of names to things, and the structure of conceptual classifications, follows specific paths, depending upon the dominant interests and guiding criteria of those cultures: for us, "snow" is snow, but for the Eskimo people there are dozens of words for snow since distinguishing the various types of snow is of vital interest to them. Thus it is only our tendency toward obviousness that makes us forget the processes that lead to the naming and identification of a thing. We assign what tends to be an unambiguous meaning to things with the aim of orienting ourselves in the world, favoring theoretical and practical knowledge, scraping away the multiple meanings of things and forgetting their symbolic and emotional values. We need only think of the symbolic and affective meanings of the fire around which tribes or families have gathered for millennia to discuss the events of the day and to recount legends and fables, or, in other cultures, the stove, which in seventeenth-century China was even deified, becoming "the Stove God," symbol of the unity of the family and the social rank of those who possessed it.[10] Unlike the warmth of a modern heater, which gives us no pleasure and evokes no fantasies when we look at it, the flame of a fire cannot be reduced to a simple phenomenon of combustion; the stove, seen as a god in China, cannot be reduced to merely a source of heat. Flame and heat certainly obey precise physical laws, but those do not exhaust its meaning.

Learning to Distinguish

Is it illusory to imagine that in the temporal interstices between sleeping and waking it is easier to catch things "from behind," as if by surprise, before they take on a precise mental and physical location? Or is it rather a matter of a disingenuous movement, similar to when children suddenly turn around to see if their guardian angel really exists? In any case, what theoretical strategies should we use to give to the world a fuller meaning, less flattened by our daily routine or less focused on maintaining control over objects? The musical notation "almost a fantasy" (a *fantasia* or fantasy is a piece of instrumental music in which the imagination of the composer takes precedence over conventional styles and forms) with which I opened this book not only indicates the presence of a vague surplus of meaning that has yet to be allocated, that shines through before things have been normalized in the passage from the logic of sleep to the logic of waking, or from darkness to light; it also shows that fantasy constitutes an essential factor in our relationship with things. Fantasy accompanies the incessant variation of our projections on the world; it reelaborates the multiple meanings that our species has inserted into things. This note of caution is necessary not in order to fabricate the eulogy of the reenchantment of the world or to propose a regression to animism but rather to adhere to the very nature of things.

I have chosen to focus on the moment of waking—to all appearances, so insignificant—precisely to facilitate our understanding of the meaning of things before habit and function take over. Nevertheless, this experience is sufficient only to make plausible the idea that this moment injects into things a virtual and indefinite multiplicity of meanings; it does not explain how this comes about. To understand this, we must in the first place analytically reconstruct an appropriate vocabulary, one capable not only of showing how symbolic, cognitive, and affective meanings coagulate around things but also so that—as was well known by the great philosophical tradition, while we have forgotten this—these meanings do not become an inappropriate and extrinsic addition to the things with which they are associated.

The Thing

After having exercised a minimum of patience in dealing with several unavoidable philosophical issues related to the linguistic and conceptual restoration of the meaning of the terms to be used, it will be possible also to clarify better the expression "the life of things," giving a reply to the legitimate questions about how inanimate objects can have an autonomous life—how they can move, feel, or even think and act. Such a paradox is solved as soon as we dispel the misunderstanding concealed in the language of our daily life, one that often infiltrates even the most sophisticated concepts. This misunderstanding results from the lack of distinction between "thing" and "object," words that have become confused over time, causing a series of cascading misinterpretations that blur both philosophical thinking and common sense. Given our habit, which is difficult to break, of regarding these two terms as synonyms, it is legitimate to give in to common usage (even I do so, on some occasions) when we don't run the risk of opening the way to misunderstandings.

In Italian, *cosa* (and its correlates in other Romance languages) is a contraction of the Latin *causa*—that is, a thing that we hold to be so important and engaging that it can mobilize us to defend it (as shown in the expression "to fight for a cause"). The Latin word *Respublica* (literally, "public thing") does not simply indicate common property but rather the essential element of what relates to everyone in a society, what deserves to be discussed in public and, consequently, forms the basis of citizens feeling that they belong to their own community. The adjective *publica* that is added to the word *res* (thing) seems to be related to *pubes*, which in Latin indicates the full maturity of males who are capable of bearing arms, being part of the army (*populus*), and, by extension, of all citizens involved in the defense and nurturing of the common good.[11]

Cosa is, in a certain sense, the conceptual equivalent of the Greek *pragma*, of the Latin *res*, or the German *Sache* (from the verb *suchen*, to seek), words that have nothing to do with a physical object per se and not even with the current usage of the German *Ding* or the English *thing* (in contrast with their etymology, which goes back to the act of gathering together to negotiate some business or to face a decisive question) but that all inevitably contain a link not only with people but also with the collective dimension of debating and deliberating. *Pragma*, *Sache*, and *res* (and, originally, *Ding* and *thing*) all refer to the essence of what we speak about or what we think and feel because we are interested in it. *Res*, which retains the same root of the Greek word *eiro* (to speak) and of the Latin *rhetor* (orator, speechmaker), therefore refers to what we discuss because we are involved in it.

The term *pragma* in Greek has a range of meanings that include the idea of an issue or matter that has to do with me, something in which I find myself implicated in my daily life, a subject to discuss and to decide especially in court or in an assembly, taking care of something, a "deal" (in Italian, a deal is called an *affare*, in the sense of something to be done). The most relevant compound words based on this term are, in the field of politics, *apragmosyne* (abstaining from political life; not only was this attitude despised but, during certain periods and in certain nations, forbidden under pain of death) and *polypragmosyne* (which by contrast designates getting excessively involved in too many things, embroiling oneself in other people's business via the intriguing of others).

In the language of philosophy, the term *pragma* was inserted by Aristotle into the expression *auto to pragma—the thing itself*, which has a specific, pregnant meaning. It indicates both facts as they effectively stand, apart from the names that are used in debating them,[12] as well as the process by which the "truth itself" constrains our thoughts to go in a certain direction:

. . . when men became joined to that point, things themselves opened the road to them, and constrained them to continue searching.[13]

Hegel's expression *die Sache selbst* is clearly modeled on Aristotle's *auto to pragma*,[14] as is Husserl's motto "*Zu den Sachen selbst!*" ("to the things themselves!")—an exhortation to focus on things themselves rather than on what has been said about them. Husserl's argument echoes Aristotle's: "We do not at all want to settle for 'pure and simple words' [that is, a purely symbolic understanding of words]. . . . Meanings that are revived from distant, confused intuitions, from indirect intuitions, cannot be sufficient for us. We want to return to things themselves."[15]

In any case, such a return presupposes the opposite journey, from intentioned contents to the analysis of concepts, metaphors, and symbols that enable us to understand them: "*Zu den Sachen und zurück*" ("to things and back").[16]

Aristotle's *auto to pragma* and Hegel's *Sache selbst* are both linked to the idea of *vis veri*, the existence of an instinct for truth that compels men to search for it. Hegel affirms this forcefully, quoting Dante, who compares the human intellect to a wild animal that returns to its lair:

I now see clearly that our intellect
cannot be satisfied until that truth enlighten it
beyond whose boundary no further truth extends.
In that truth, like a wild beast in its den, it rests
once it has made its way there—and it can do that,
or else its every wish would be in vain.[17]

The *vis veri*, the *auto to pragma*, and the *Sache selbst* set the stage for the unraveling of a skein of meanings related to the essence of a thing. In an apparently passive manner, thought has only to assist in the process. In fact, these terms relate to the automatic unfolding of meaning, which has the ability to articulate and explain itself, by itself.

All of this takes place in contrast to the road taken by individual consciousness, which slowly and tortuously approaches the understanding of the essence of a thing, in a process that originates from the subjective sphere and is defined as "by us" (*pros emas*) by Aristotle and, in another obvious reference, *für uns* by Hegel. The *auto to pragma* and the *Sache selbst* represent, instead, the concise, "rectilinear," logically linked process of reasoning that takes as its point of departure axioms or indemonstrable principles—just the opposite of "by us," which is a process of dealing with all the random occurrences and ramblings that are characteristic of a subjectivity that is not yet in tune with the truth.

The most powerful and coherent model of *auto to pragma* is provided by Euclid's *Elements*, where, in the demonstration of a theorem, it is as if the thing itself, propelled by the *vis veri*, progressively revealed its essence to anyone who is disposed to follow the steps imposed by Euclid's method (*meta odos*, a prescribed route through which one arrives at results). In his *Phenomenology of Spirit*, Hegel, too, shows how, in order to grasp the movement of a thing itself, it is necessary "to watch," delving into and losing oneself in the object in order to express its intimate essence: "Philosophical understanding demands that we abandon ourselves [*sich übergeben*] to the life of the object or—which amounts to the same thing—that we have it present in our minds and express its interior need."[18] The knowledge that is obtained from this process does not coincide at all with the mimetic reproduction of the object in the traditional, passive mirror of the mind, with which a subject separated from the world would be endowed. For Hegel, a subject is activity; it is energy that does not content itself with the kind of static equilibrium typical of the "horizontal" subject-object relationship represented by "substance." If, to indicate the exigency of a dynamic rupture of this kind of equilibrium, Hegel referred in his early writings to the "union of the union and of the non-union," in his *Phenomenology of Spirit* the indissoluble link between the subject and the object is subjected to the definitive primacy of subjectivity: "everything depends on understanding and expressing truth not as *substance*, but just as decisively as *subject*."[19]

The concepts of *rem tene*, *verba sequentur*, and *res ipsa* also relate to this model of the automatic unfolding of a thing: "If you have grasped the essential nucleus of your argument, the words will come by themselves"; "the thing speaks for itself." It is obvious that, in rigorous terms, an object external to our consciousness is incapable of speaking; in grasping the thing, in going beyond the mute object, our thoughts give voice to the "substance," to what nourishes it in the process of understanding. For that matter, the Greek term *ousia* (substance) originally denoted the little field from which the farmer drew not his substance but his sustenance. The Spanish word *res* still retains an analogous meaning: "ox," an essential beast of burden for the survival of a farmer's family. From as early as the time of the ancient Greek poet Hesiod, the household or *oikos*—the house and family taken together— was made up of the "master who commands," the "woman," and the "plower ox."[20]

Auto to pragma and *Sache selbst* are distinguished from *pragma* and *Sache* (as well as from *res* and *causa*) precisely because they insist on the process of automatic unfolding of a truth that has been reached, that speaks in the first person; the other expressions refer above all to the moment of discussion and discovery in which the thing incorporates its attributes and progressively takes shape in both theory and practice.

In Hegel, the sense of *Sache* and *Sache selbst* takes another form, which, however, retains the nucleus of the meanings that are present in other contexts and authors. Hegel shows how an individual realizes himself through action but also, armed by the presumption of being the only one to escape from the bad faith and corruption of others, purports to represent the "common cause" (*Sache selbst*), whereas in reality he represents nothing but his own limited interest, his own private cause (*Sache*). The *Sache selbst*, which is the result of each and every person's actions, is in fact the anonymous result that everyone would like to make their own, in a sort of Hobbesian war that everyone wages against everyone else—a war that takes place on the field of "the animal realm of the spirit," where the individual does not realize that he has been conditioned by the historical world and therefore acts as if he found himself in a simple, natural environment. Unlike animal societies—such as those of bees or ants—in which a collective order of spontaneous cooperation reigns, human beings (and this is their greatness as well as their misfortune) are not spontaneously predisposed toward the interest of society.

As shown by the models that Hegel had in mind—the transfiguration of private vices into public virtues as in Mandeville, the *concordia discors* (discordant harmony) of Kant, and the "invisible hand" of Adam Smith—unexpected effects arise from the pursuit of one's own advantage because reciprocal hostility and competitiveness tend to set in motion the mobilization of an individual's energies and the growth and maturation of that individual. Surrounded on all sides by his fellow human beings—who aspire to obtain the same scarce rewards for which he himself strives—each individual is constrained to ascend, to stretch upward like a plant that has no space to expand horizontally. Thus in modern societies based on individualism and competition, human beings are situated somewhere between the animal nature of their needs and the loftier exigencies of cooperation in society. As soon as the *Sache selbst* gains its own autonomy—becoming an objective "compenetration" of individuality and effective reality—the self-deception of anyone who purports to personify the common cause evaporates. As they converge, the multiple private causes transcend their own particularities and rise to the collective level of the *Geist* ("spirit," in the sense of "universal labor of the human species," i.e., civilization). This arises as an extension of the *Sache selbst*, and, in an unending movement toward the common good, overcomes the contradictions in which the strivings of individuals become entangled.[21] In *Phenomenology of Spirit*, the actions of each and every individual flow together, forming the "ethical substance"—a public, mental, and affective space that is the basis of a particular civilization. This substance is capable of directing the actions of individuals because, as it is separated from their private intentions and becomes objective, it is endowed with a transcendent value and exemplarity. This is the case with the "unwritten laws" of Antigone and the laws promulgated by Creon's *polis*.

More generally, outside of the ethical dimension, so-called classical metaphysics reduced objects to their logically essential elements, to their concept:

> The older metaphysics . . . presupposed as its principle that only what is known of things and in things by thought is really true in them, that is, what is known in them not in their immediacy but as first elevated to the form of thinking, as things for thought. This metaphysics thus held that thinking and the determination of thinking are not something alien to the subject matters, but are rather their essence, or that the *thing* and the *thinking* of them agree in and for themselves . . . ; that

thinking in its immanent determinations, and the true nature of things, are one and the same content.[22]

In Hegel, this kind of metaphysics is fundamentally transformed into an ontology, a system capable of unifying being and thought. Thus Hegel is not satisfied with knowing, as in Kant, the phenomena that are manifested to the senses and the intellect by means of a mysterious "thing in itself" (*Ding an sich*); he wants to know effective reality, to make it speak in the language of the *Sache selbst*. On a logical level, the ontology is articulated in categories (with concepts like "becoming," "equal," or "different") that support not only all of our representations but also every content and orientation of our mind, because they are the "adamantine net—if we wish—in which we carry all material and by which alone we make it intelligible."[23]

Between Object and Subject

"Object" is a more recent term than "thing," originating in medieval scholasticism; it seems to derive theoretically from the Greek term *problema*, where "problem" is understood as an obstacle put forward as a form of defense, an impediment that blocks the way and causes something to stop. In Latin, more precisely, *obicere* means to throw against or place before.

Thus the idea of *objectum* (or, in German, *Gegenstand*—what is before or against me) implies a challenge, a contraposition that prevents the subject's immediate affirmation precisely because it "objects" to the subject's pretentions to dominance. It presupposes a confrontation that concludes with a definitive overpowering of the object, which, after the struggle between subject and object, is made available to be possessed and manipulated by the subject. A thing, in contrast, is not an object, an indeterminate obstacle that I find before me and that I have to conquer or circumvent—rather, it is a cluster of relationships in which I feel and know that I am implicated and of which I do not want to have exclusive control. None of these expressions—*pragma*, *res*, *causa*, or *Sache*—refers to objects in a specific, exclusive way, but each one relates to logic, to seeking, to praxis, or to human relationships.

As is well known, the word "subject" originally had a meaning that was diametrically opposed to the meaning that we usually attribute to it today: it designated precisely what we now call an "object." The Latin *subjectum* translates the Greek *hypokeimenon* and denotes the substrate that supports the qualities or the mutations of a material (or, in a logical sense, the predicates of a subject). From Aristotle to the medieval scholastic authors, "subject" meant that to which determinations are attributed or to which such determinations are inherent. To be even more technically precise, it is the real object to which the predicable determinations refer (as happens in Aristotle's *Metaphysics*, where "the subject is that thing about which everything can be said, but which, in its turn, cannot be said about anything");[24] it is the substance in which qualities or determinations are inherent.[25] For Locke, too, "subject" still designated the substratum or support.[26]

Although Descartes still uses the terms "subject" and "object" in the scholastic sense (and what most resembles subjectivity is what he calls *sola mens* in the third *Meditation*), he is considered the initiator of modern subjectivity. In reality, when the inaugural gesture of modernity is attributed to Descartes, what is being considered is his famous formula "I think, therefore I am" as the incontrovertible evidence that is the foundation of all knowledge. But starting with his youthful admission that he is playing a part in the great theater of the world ("*larvatus prodeo*": "I go forward masked"), Descartes is frequently presented as an astute Pro-

metheus who gives men the gifts of rationality and the freedom
to choose on the basis of rational evidence.

In reality, it is a matter of an objective that Descartes considered to be too ambitious. Only with Kant, and above all after
Kant, does "subjectivity" become synonymous with individual
consciousness and autonomy. Yet, in spite of the fact that the distinction between the two poles of subjectivity and objectivity has
now been stabilized, it can still happen that the meanings of the
terms "subjective" and "objective" become reversed. This holds,
above all, in reference to contemporary mass societies and their
conformism:

> Objective means the non-controversial aspect of things, their
> unquestioned impression, the façade made up of classified
> data, that is, the subjective; and they call subjective anything
> which breaches that façade, engages the specific experience of
> a matter, casts off all ready-made judgements and substitutes
> relatedness to the object for the majority consensus of those
> who do not even look at it, let alone think about it—that is,
> the objective.[27]

Orphan Objects

The meaning of "thing" is broader than that of "object" because
it also includes people or ideals and, more generally, everything
that interests us and is close to our heart (or that can be discussed
in public because it touches on the common good, from which,
paradoxically, the good of the individual also depends). Keeping
people necessarily in the background, I have chosen here to speak
only about "material" things that are designed, constructed, or
invented by human beings using the raw materials provided by

nature according to specific cultural models, techniques, and traditions. Privileging material objects over human subjects also serves to show the subject itself overturned, in its most hidden and least-frequented aspect. Invested with emotions, concepts, and symbols that are projected onto them by individuals, society, and history, objects become things, distinguishing themselves from merchandise, which is merely an object with a value that can be used or exchanged or serve as a status symbol. (Later in this book, I will deal at some length with merchandise, and not only to contrast objects that are merchandise with "things.")

One wonders if it is possible to devise a classification of the virtually infinite multiplicity of objects, merchandise, and things that surround us, especially today, when "everyday objects . . . proliferate, needs multiply, production speeds up the life-span of such objects—yet we lack the vocabulary to name them all."[28] How does the transubstantiation of objects into things occur? How does one pass from indifference or ignorance of something, to thinking about it, perceiving it, or imagining it as endowed with a plurality of meanings, capable of emitting its own implications?

Similar to the diagnostic technique of Quantitative Magnetic Color Imaging (QMCI) of the brain or other organs, it would be wonderful to have virtual maps of every individual—maps that would show the aspects of reality that interest each person most at a given time. The areas of their greatest cognitive and emotional involvement could be drawn in red, and different gradations and streaks of gray would indicate areas of less interest or none at all. We would have "identity cards" that would make it possible to follow the process that transforms objects into sounding boards that resonate with our ideas, activities, passions, and fantasies.

Like the dry twig described by Stendhal in *De l'amour* (which, left for some time in the salt mines of Salzburg, becomes covered with splendid crystals—an allegory for the qualities that the lover's mind projects onto the beloved person), any object is susceptible to infusions and removals of meanings, positive and negative, of being surrounded with an aura or being deprived of one, of becoming encrusted with crystals of thought and emotion, or of turning back into a dry twig, enriching or impoverishing our world by adding or subtracting values and meanings.

We invest objects intellectually and emotionally, we give them sentimental meanings and qualities, we place them in coffers of desire or envelop them in repellent coverings, we situate them within systems of relationships, we insert them into stories that we tell about ourselves or others.

Things are not just things, they bear human traces, they prolong the memory of people for us. In their modest, loyal way, objects that have long accompanied us are no less faithful than the animals and plants around us. Each has its history and a significance that has melded with that of the people who used and loved it. Objects and people together form a sort of unity that cannot be painlessly separated.[29]

But how do the projection and distortion of our emotional investments onto objects function, and from what do they derive? The answer, with results that are still persuasive to a great extent today, was sketched out by Sigmund Freud in his famous essay "Mourning and Melancholia." We invest people, animals, ideals, or objects with libidinal energy of differing intensities, and this energy strictly adheres to its object. If the object should disappear from the horizon of our life (because of the death of a loved one, the destruction of an ideal, or the disappearance of a thing that meant a great deal to us), this libidinal energy, no longer anchored to what used to attract and hold it, wanders aimlessly in search of a new place and, not finding it, reacts impulsively, trying to force the psyche incapable of hosting it to invest it again somewhere else.

The aversion to disengaging itself from the earlier connection (because it would seem to be an act of unfaithfulness that would betray the memory of that connection) can, nevertheless, impede this fluctuating energy for a long time from finding another object of love upon which to fix itself. Then a mournful state of mind is created, causing an interior void and leading to a painful loss of interest in the world. In the case of melancholia, the individual turns against himself through processes of self-blame.[30]

Such a sense of the transience of everything is powerfully expressed by Fernando Pessoa:

> I experience time as a terrible ache. I get ridiculously upset whenever I have to leave anything: the miserable little rented room where I spent a few months, the table in the provincial hotel at which I dined on each of my six days there, even the waiting room at the railway station where I wasted two hours waiting for the train. But the good things of life, when I have to leave them and think, with all the sensitivity my nerves can muster, that I will never see or have them again, at least not as they are in that exact, precise moment, hurt me metaphysically. An abyss yawns open in my soul and a cold blast from the hour of God brushes my pale face.
>
> Time! The past! What I was and will never be again! What I had and will never have again! The Dead! The dead who loved me when I was a child. When I remember them my whole soul grows cold and I feel myself to be an exile from every heart, alone in the night of my own self, crying like a beggar at the closed silence of every door.[31]

In the end, however, we often emerge from a situation of mourning when our libido finds a substitute—a new object, or one that previously had little or no importance for us, as when an elderly widow overcompensates for the death of her husband by lavishing excessive affection on a pet dog, or when someone who has lost his or her political or religious faith embraces another faith with great ardor, turning against the preceding one, with a surplus of zeal that is the unquestionable sign of the struggle that he or she has had and continues to have against his or her own past.

Every person "manages" a certain amount of libido: to use a financial metaphor, it is like managing a portfolio of investments (in the form of bank deposits, stocks, or real properties) that gives one security and the composition of which does not change a great deal, at least as long as things are going well. Outside of the metaphor, the totality of libidinal investments reflects the coordinates of each person's relationship with the world, the intentional connections between the individual and objects. These relationships anticipate the formation of a critical consciousness, as always happens in the relationship between an infant and its mother, or as sometimes occurs with children who form attachments to a blanket or a doll, for example. Affections precede concepts, to later become intertwined with them.

When the connection between a person and an object is broken—either because of the death of the former or the loss of the latter—the aversion toward accepting the loss of what we love reveals our futile but heroic protest against the irreversibility of time. Not being able to keep things once they are lost, we search for surrogates, shifting our emotional and cognitive investments elsewhere. This explains, at least in part, the waning or waxing of significance and value that things undergo because of our incessant and often unconscious incorporation of meanings into objects or our dismissal of them. Objects are either transformed into things or downgraded from the status of things to become indifferent entities.

The same phenomenon of emotional and intellectual investment occurs when, through a deviation, our emotion is focused on a transactional object that acts as an intermediary and diverts our emotion onto other targets. For example, grief can be attenuated by funerary rituals and monuments, which, though intended to be remembrances of the deceased, in reality contribute to our forgetting those who have died: "with the expression of sorrow, in the various forms of celebration and the cult of the dead, the feeling of agony is overcome, because it is objectified. Thus, as we try to keep the dead alive, we begin to make them effectively die inside us."[32] But the loss of something or someone we love is always terrible. And going through the motions of mourning does not always compensate for it: every loss is an anticipatory tolling of the final bell; it mimics, in an attenuated form, the moment when we ourselves will have to leave everything behind.

One specific way of going through the motions of mourning, which also involves objects, occurs when we take stock of what remains in our parents' home after they die. This is when we follow the tracks of their existence, now concluded, and review their past emotional investments, embodied in objects that had meaning for them and not (or not yet) for us.

> What was the value of this trinket, this scarf, this watercolour that my parents had never made me a gift of, of this dictionary which would have been useful to my children, which they had deemed not good enough to give me, of this flask they could have given me with a smile and that I now received unsmiling?[33]

There exists, in general, an enormous quantity of "orphaned objects," left behind by their previous owners, which we are called upon to adopt, reject, or ignore. There is a sort of *translatio imperii* or metempsychosis that causes objects to pass from hand to hand so that their life can continue even after the death or departure of whoever owned them. Through legal documents such as wills, or through purchases, or by simple discovery, objects become material links of continuity between generations, something that can be enjoyed by turns.

> Objects live several times over, but once passed on to new owners, do they keep any trace of their former life? It is no matter of indifference to imagine them elsewhere, in other hands, for uses that are superimposed on those they previously had. . . . Things are not so different from people or animals. Objects have a soul. I felt as though I were responsible for protecting them from too dismal a fate.[34]

Wood and Stone

The erogation of libidinal energy on objects can, in certain circumstances, become transformed into fetishism. In a sort of synecdoche (*pars pro toto*—part for whole), an article of clothing or a photograph can become charged with an all-encompassing erotic significance, an excess of meaning or—in the case of the African idols that gave their name to the phenomenon of fetishism[35]—of cultural and religious meanings in general.

The question that preoccupied the Catholic missionaries in western Africa—why objects (sometimes covered with incrustations of vegetable oils, egg, or blood) can be adored—has been proposed again by contemporary anthropology.

In the populations that live around the Gulf of Benin, the fetish is where spirits take up their dwelling, where raw material becomes the support for symbols: "The unthinkable and, in a certain way, power, are on the side of raw inertia, pure materiality. What is natural is therefore life, and this leads us to think that what is supernatural is on the side of the inert." If, as Pascal asserted, "man is a thinking reed," then what is a "non-thinking reed? It is in any case unthinkable, and, for our consciousness, frightening, scandalous, impossible." Animism, apparently the diametric opposite of brute matter, is in part complementary to it. If Lévi-Strauss was right when he maintained that, from the moment that language was born, the universe was inevitably charged with meaning, articulated, and diversified, then precisely because "intelligence needs a minimum of difference and distinction, it is necessary [to attribute] a little bit of life to the object of intelligence." As a result, if "the unthinkable is pure material, mineral homogeneity," then it is obligatory "to animate it in order to understand it, to begin to think of it. The 'fetishists,' it was said with amazement, adore 'wood and stone.' They have no choice: they think."[36]

African fetishism evokes the wonder and consternation that we should experience in the face of the inanimate, the material of which objects are composed. Objects belong to another world than the one that living things inhabit, a world in itself, mysterious and evocative, as is the transformation of a living body into a cadaver, a world with which it is possible to communicate, in the religious sphere, only through the language of the sacred. We also learn from fetishism that "in man's efforts to understand the world, he always disposes of a surplus of signification (which he shares out among things in accordance with the laws of the symbolic thinking which it is the task of ethnologists and linguists to study)."[37] This "surplus of signification," I should add, is distributed among things in different, unequal ways, leaving in each an unanalyzable residue, a bundle of unsaturated bonds and allusions that are ineffable (not because they cannot be said but because one would never finish saying them) to that which cannot yet be thought.

The Memory of Things

From prehistoric utensils made of stone, bone, or wood to the first ceramic products, from the earliest machines to today's robots, objects have traveled a long road together with our species. Changing with the times, places, and modalities of production, depending on diverse histories and traditions, things are always slowly or suddenly invested with new values and enveloped in new auras of meaning. With greater or lesser awareness, we all confer meaning on things, but only artists do so methodically and according to their own personal techniques and paths of experimentation. Artists give their own voice to mute things, and sometimes, as happens frequently with children, they even pretend that things can speak. This is the case with Carducci in the poem *Davanti a San Guido*, or with the thirteenth-century poet Guido Cavalcanti, who gives a voice to his tools for writing and erasing:

> we sad, despondent quills,
> sorrowing scissors and knife
> have written in anguish these words you've heard
>
> now we speak to you leaving
> and coming to your presence: the hand moving us feels
> doubtful things appear in the heart.[38]

Every generation is surrounded by a particular landscape of objects that define an epoch through the patinas, signs, and atmosphere of the time in which they were created and modified. In their own way, objects grow or perish, like plants and animals; they go on for years or centuries; they are looked after, cared for or neglected, forgotten, destroyed.

When they become obsolete, objects end up in basements, cellars, pawnshops, in junk stores or antique shops, in landfills.

Whether they are found or purchased, they emanate an effluvium of melancholy; they are like withered flowers that need our attention in order to revive.

The typology and meaning of objects were described by Walter Benjamin in reference to the creature Odradek in Kafka's short story "The Cares of a Family Man," where they become the enigmatic allegory of the progressive oblivion to which the character of the father is subjected.[39] The Odradek resembles "a flat star-shaped spool for thread" that "lurks by turns in the garret, the stairway, the lobbies, the entrance hall." At times, the spool disappears for months on end:

Then he has presumably moved into other houses; but he always comes faithfully back to our house again. . . . Am I to suppose, then, that he will always be rolling down the stairs, with ends of thread trailing after him, right before the feet of my children, and my children's children? He does no harm to anyone that one can see; but the idea that he is likely to survive me I find almost painful.[40]

The ubiquity of the spool known as Odradek and its intermittent reappearances allude to the unsituability of the figure of the father when the spool disappears, and the broken threads refer to what it would be possible to reunite, in memory, reestablishing an emotional continuity. This kind of emotional continuity is arduous, as seen in the famous "Letter to His Father," where Kafka says that his father Hermann has accused him of being cold, distant, and ungrateful, and he in his turn reproaches his father for his psychological violence and intimidations.

The taxonomy and the mutations of this type of entity have been described in detail by Francesco Orlando in *Gli oggetti desueti nelle immagini della letteratura* and by Umberto Eco in the illustrated novel *The Mysterious Flame of Queen Loana*.

Orlando finds in the "jumble of objects" and of things that are apparently "useless or out of date or strange" that they have lost their usefulness and have become "anti-merchandise," a typology that (through the testimonies of literature, especially the literature of the last three centuries) clarifies human beings' relationship with the physical world that has been subjugated by them, on the borderline between culture and nature, in the process of transformation of that world, not to mention their relationship "with time, which leaves its mark on things: projecting onto things the limits of both the metahistorical human condition, and of the historical duration of civilization."[41]

Among the innumerable texts quoted by Orlando, a poem by Borges entitled "*Las cosas*" ("Things") stands out:

My cane, my pocket change, this ring of keys
The obedient lock, the belated notes
The few days left to me will not find time
To read, the deck of cards, the tabletop,
A book, and crushed in its pages the withered
Violet, monument to an afternoon
Undoubtedly unforgettable, now forgotten,
The mirror in the west where a red sunrise
Blazes its illusion. How many things,
Files, doorsills, atlases, wine glasses, nails,
Serve us like slaves who never say a word,
Blind and so mysteriously reserved.
They will endure beyond our vanishings;
And they will never know that we have gone.[42]

Remaining within the purview of Latin American literature, I would add here the last stanza of Pablo Neruda's long, detailed poem "*Oda a las cosas*" ("Ode to Things"):

Oh irrevocable
river
of things
it won't be said
that I only
loved
fish
or plants of the jungle and meadow,
that I only
loved
what jumps,
survives or sighs.
It's not true:
many things
told me all.
Not only did they touch me,
or my hand touched them,
but they accompanied
my life
in such a way,
that they existed with me,
and were so alive
that they lived with me half my life,
and will die with me half my death.[43]

For Umberto Eco, on the other hand, old cigarette packs, post-cards, postage stamps, or comic books refer not only to personal memories of childhood or adolescence or to events common to a people and an epoch (in the case of Eco, to the period of fascism, the Second World War, and the early years of the Italian Republic). They are also documents endowed with intrinsic dignity, capable of evoking clusters of memories and a mass of information useful for the understanding not only of material history but also of history *tout court*. In general terms, by becoming transformed into a thing after a long interregnum of oblivion, an object manifests not only the traces of the natural and social processes that have produced it but also the ideas, the prejudices, the trends, and the tastes of an entire society.

From Obviousness to Discovery

It is no longer necessary to rely solely on imagination to grasp the value of things in all their complexity and to peruse their layers of meaning. But it is necessary to suspend the obvious, to discover in things the capacity to deliver a surplus of meanings that not even habit, ignorance, neglect, or the frequent intellectual and emotional malnutrition of individuals can succeed in eliminating completely.

It is not easy to renounce the obvious—one has to make an effort to bring about not only the conversion of one's intellect but also of one's will. It is true that our perspective is never totally innocent, but it is just as true that

What makes a subject difficult to understand—if it is significant, important—is not that some special instruction about abstruse things is necessary to understand it. Rather it is the contrast between the understanding of the subject and what most people want to see. Because of this the very things that are most obvious can become more difficult to understand. What has to be overcome is not difficulty of the intellect but of the will.[44]

And it is also true that "the aspects of things that are most important for us are hidden because of their simplicity and familiarity. (One is unable to notice something—because it is always before one's eyes.)"[45] Once learned, the new qualities absorbed by our will, our intellect, and our perception become somatic, generating a paradoxical spontaneity, like that of a pianist who, after long, hard study, seems to move his fingers on the keys effortlessly and without having to look at the score.

Going beyond the obvious, sweeping away the dust of banality and oblivion that conceals the nature and the history of things, is not only possible; in fact, it constitutes the premise of every act of exploration and discovery. Etymologically, "obvious" (*obvius*) is used to denote a thing that is found along the way or a person who is accessible, close to hand, who doesn't demand great effort to approach or to grant confidence. To enter into the realm of the obvious, it suffices to choose a path that is not obstructed by *problemata*, moving tranquilly toward something that we presume we already know or are capable of recognizing easily.

But who can assure us that we really know what we believe is known or evident? Reality does not take refuge behind the variety of what we can perceive with our senses and does not always seek asylum in the remote realm of ideas. It hides above all behind the obvious, in the incongruous clusters of sensory, emotional, or conceptual data that block or at least slow down our mental metabolism. Liberation from what is known has long been the goal of the most disparate theories and practices, which have constantly sought to pass from the *obvius* to the *abvius*, from the routine to what takes us outside of the routine, off the beaten path. Indirectly, these theories and practices ask how our "world" came about and by which paths and side roads it has become obvious to us, erasing any sense of wonder as we regard it. The concept of a sense of wonder that is not devoid of disquietude—*thaumazein*—is at the very root of philosophy—in Plato's *Theaetetus* (155d) and Aristotle's *Metaphysics* (I, 2, 982 b, 11–24)—precisely where the task of divesting the world of its obviousness takes place, without the pretense of making everything absolutely clear.

To leave the obvious behind, it is necessary to undertake voyages of discovery. Giving up an advantageous position is rewarded by perceiving, in a nebulous way, that something is beginning to stir in our spirit, taking on the colors of a feeling mingled with joy, hope, and disquietude. At the beginning we don't yet know where we should go and what we should search for, so we assist ourselves with tools that we intuitively think are promising: provisional mental bridges, metaphors, combinations of images and concepts; we look for symmetries and formal elegance, variations in perspective.

Although the journey was initially entrusted to fragile hypotheses, when the search is successful, we are amazed that, by ability or luck, we have gotten to where we are. Looking back, the road we have taken now seems to have been the only right way to go, a *via regia* like the one indicated by Euclid in his *Elements*, a result that has always existed and that only needed to be made explicit, because—as Mozart said about music—"everything has already been composed but not yet transcribed." From the moment in which the result has been reached, in exposing it, it seems that the thing itself has revealed its meaning, according to laws of intimate necessity.

Although they appear suddenly, in reality even the mental flashes that we experience in this journey arise from subterranean workings. The spark of discovery—not only for a scientist or an artist but in each one of us when it comes to the solution of certain of our problems—is preceded by a long period of preparation. A compelling example of this kind of process is the discovery of the formula for benzene by the German chemist Friedrich August Kekulé. After having pondered for fifteen years how to connect six carbon atoms with six hydrogen atoms without violating the laws of chemical valence, one day, while sleeping in front of the fireplace, Kekulé dreamed that he saw snakes devouring each others' tails, forming a circle. He then understood that the carbon atoms form a hexagonal ring with alternating single and double links, each of which contains its own carbon atom. Passing from "for us" to "the thing itself," the rocky road opened up onto a panoramic expanse: Kekulé had arrived at the nature of benzene—the goal of his laborious research.

To discover or invent something, it is not sufficient to recognize the nature of the phenomena that are encountered; thousands of scientists and students had seen what is now known as the Golgi apparatus under the microscope, yet no one had identified it before Camillo Golgi did so, in 1897.[46] It is also necessary to know how to proceed in a counterintuitive direction, to turn common sense on its head and abandon age-old prejudices, like the Montgolfier brothers and the Wright brothers, when they proved that man can fly; like the German-Austrian furniture maker and *ébéniste* Michael Thonet, who—ideally confuting Kant, who spoke of the unmodifiable "bent wood" of the human race—succeeded in curving beechwood by warming it with steam inside of cast-iron forms; like Thomas Edison, who invented incandescent light by burning metal filaments in a vacuum rather than by lighting a flame fueled by oxygen, as had always been done up to that time.

Intentionality and Objects

The skeptical suspension of judgment, Cartesian doubts, and Husserl's phenomenology are all forms of cessation of obviousness. To limit ourselves to an example from the twentieth century, for Husserl this task was entrusted to the *epoché* (ἐποχή, *epokhē*, "suspension")—that is, the suspension of our natural attitude. The attitude of *epoché* does not modify the object but instead modifies our way of considering the object and invites us to regain our sense of wonder and innocence (in the language of the gospels, not to be, but to become like children).

Consciousness is always consciousness of something; consciousness does not exist on one side and the object on the other. There is always an "intentional" connection—with two poles, inseparable and constitutive—a connection that precedes the separation of the consciousness and the object. We are not detached from the world, and there is no subject that is added *a posteriori* to an object. Indeed, the sense of intentionality resides precisely in the mutual belonging of consciousness and object.

Through the theory of intentionality, Husserl behaved, in a certain sense, like the Romans during the First Punic War. Inexpert in naval warfare, the Romans invented the *rostrum*, a boarding bridge that they attached to Carthaginian ships so that they could board their enemies' vessels and engage in hand-to-hand combat as if they were on land. In a similar way, Husserl transported the object onto the terrain of consciousness and consciousness onto the terrain of the object, creating a common space of integration and exploration. This enabled him to oppose the tendency of the modern natural sciences, which have made subjectivity into an abstraction.[47]

According to Merleau-Ponty, the natural sciences have practiced "a thinking which looks on [the object] from above,"[48] tending to disregard its individual diversities and focusing on its homogeneous universality. Under the pretext of extending this model to every form of knowledge and consciousness, the natural sciences have expunged the activity of the subject, considering it with detachment as an object like any other, without seeing the tight network of cognitive and emotional relationships of which every subject is the hub. Instead of keeping a tolerant openness toward the plurality of meanings of experience and taking into consideration the diverse levels of meaning of reality, the natural sciences tend to force every object to recline on Procrustes' "standard"-sized bed.[49]

Renouncing subjectivity, the logic that supports the natural sciences proposes to contrast the opacity of unreflected experience, without being conscious of the fact that subjectivity itself cannot be reduced to an object, and without recognizing, as Husserl explained in his *Cartesian Meditations*, that the ego eludes any objectification because it is capable of transcending it.[50] In the effort to find a life that is different from the one that is extinguished by the Medusa of the objectifying sciences, which have canceled life's polysemy and individual qualities, Husserl distinguished two worlds: one that is the result of the expunging of the subject by the object and that operates via the category of cause, and another captured in "a horizon of things that are not bodies, but rather objects of value." This latter world not only reintroduces the subject but also habituates it "to think, to evaluate, to desire, and to act" on the basis of the category of motivation, thus making the object itself speak "in the first person."

For some critics, Husserl's phenomenological approach is a failure because ultimately he did not immunize himself against the evil that he had denounced, forgetting the very subjectivity that he sought to save:

Like the photographer of old, the phenomenologist wraps himself with the black veil of his ἐποχή, implores the objects to hold still and unchanging and ultimately realizes passively and without spontaneity of the knowing subject, family portraits of the sort of that mother "who glances lovingly at her little flock."[51]

Albeit from a different perspective, Bachelard, too, accuses Husserl's phenomenology of continuing to be imbued with naturalism, in that it presupposes that objects offer themselves to our perception in a passive, ingenuous way, as if the knowing subject did not play any role. Bachelard diametrically opposes phenomenology with "phenomeno-technique," through which science—human knowledge organized with the contributions of innumerable individuals—constructs the object that it studies by proceeding from the rational to the real. In this sense, for example, an electron is nothing more than a "reified theorem."[52]

But especially during the last phase of his thinking, Husserl did not run the risk denounced by Adorno. Rejecting the theory of the mind as a mirror that reflects an external reality—the *adaequatio rei ad intellectum*—Husserl firmly established, by means of intentionality, an unbreakable link between consciousness and the object. He rejected the passivity of consciousness and of the id with regard to the so-called external world. The id cannot be reduced to an inert object. In returning periodically "to things themselves," the id reveals itself as pure energy that transcends objects. The transcendence of the id could be summed up in the words that the painter Paul Klee wanted to be inscribed on his tombstone: "I cannot be caught in immanence."[53]

Husserl's program was more ambitious than his critics think; for him, for an object to be able to express itself, it must let itself become impregnated by the world, and suspend judgment (since objects give themselves not only before they are judged but also in a precategorical and prethematic manner). Thanks to the repeated effort to free oneself from habits, it appears clear that objects do not exist autonomously, by their very nature; rather, they are nodes in the tightly woven network of coordinates with which we structure the world, which, in turn, cannot be separated from consciousness because "an absolute reality is just as valid as a round square."[54]

Perception—especially visual perception—"is a continuous process" that is inexhaustible because—unlike the God envisaged by Leibniz, who sees objects from all sides at once—we perceive objects at different times, in the "continuous alteration of seeing," from one point of view at a time.[55] Since the object is never perceptible to us in its entirety, our every perception inevitably refers to our memory and imagination, which complete the object according to lines that are traced, enabling us to recognize it.[56] Even in Leopardi, incidentally, imagination provides the limits of perception, "faking" (or rather simulating) what is beyond those limits:

> Then, in place of sight, what is at work is the imagination, and the fantastic takes the place of what is real. The soul imagines what it cannot see, whatever is hidden, that tree, that hedge, that tower, and wanders in an imaginary space, and pictures things in a way that would be impossible if its view could extend in all directions, because the real would exclude the imaginary.[57]

For Husserl, "Each I finds itself as a central point, so to speak a zero-point of a system of coordinates, in reference to which the I considers, arranges, and knows all things of the world, the already known and the unknown." Thus "everyone has the same world around them, and, perhaps, many of us see the same thing, the same fragment of the world; but for everyone *the same thing* is manifested in a different way, depending upon its different position in space."[58]

In a single glance, I can take in the "verandah," the "garden," and the "children in the arbor" all at the same time, without, naturally, exhausting the other possible points of view or the world that surrounds them. Every time that "the rays of the illuminative regard of attention" are directed toward something, bringing it into the foreground, what has been focused on is necessarily surrounded by a haze, by a "mist of obscure indeterminacies." My exploration of the things that are "on hand" (*vorhanden*, or simply present) can extend from one part of space to another, without there being a privileged direction, whereas temporally it can only move bilaterally toward the past or the future:

> I can change my standpoint in space and time, turn my regard in this or that direction, forwards or backwards in time; I can always obtain new perceptions and representations, more or less clear and more or less rich in content, or else more or less clear images in which I illustrate to myself intuitionally what is possible or likely within the fixed forms of a spatial and temporal world.[59]

Objects are invested with meaning by the rays of my attention, which not only sees them with the eyes of the body but also understands them, thanks to language, with the eyes of the mind, because seeing "is an amalgam of the two—pictures and language."[60]

The world, in fact, as Husserl says,

> is continually "on hand" for me and I myself am a member of it. Moreover, this world is there for me not only as a world of things, but also with the same immediacy as a *world of objects with values, a world with goods, a practical world*. I simply find the physical things in front of me furnished not only with merely material determinations but also with value-characteristics, as beautiful and ugly, pleasant and unpleasant, agreeable and disagreeable, and the like. Immediately, physical things stand there as Objects of use, the "table" with

its "books," the "drinking glass," the "vase," the "piano," etc. These value-characteristics and practical characteristics also belong *constitutively to the objects "on hand"* as Objects, regardless of whether or not I turn to such characteristics and Objects.[61]

I who see and interrogate objects am the active element, but it is they that—as expressed in Aristotle's *Topics*—show me the way to make them "speak."

In the Shape of a Jug

The twentieth century inaugurated the first conscious attempts to rediscover the meaning of things that was concealed beneath their inert anonymity. Moving in a different direction from Husserl, in 1911 Georg Simmel began a tradition that would be continued in 1918 by Ernst Bloch and would culminate, in 1958, with Martin Heidegger. Albeit starting from different premises and arriving at different conclusions, all three philosophers considered ordinary objects such as a bowl, a vase, or a jug as a crossroads of relationships that do not reduce an object to its necessary material substance, nor to the basic conceptual framework that defines it.

Simmel's attention was focused, on the one hand, on the distinction between the physical and symbolic space of objects and, on the other hand, on the compenetration of internal and external, symbol and material. The first aspect refers to the fact that the handle and the jug have, in real space, innumerable possible connections with whatever surrounds them, whereas when they are depicted by a painter, they enter into a closed, self-referential space, compressed into a single esthetic vision. The second aspect, instead, emphasizes the cobelonging of the spiritual element and the physical element in man's relationship with things:

> But the bowl is not simply held in the palm of the hand; it is grasped by the handle. Thus a mediating bridge is formed, a pliable joining of the hand with the bowl, which, with a palpable continuity, transmits the impulse of the soul into the bowl, into its manipulation. But then, though the reflux of this energy, the bowl is drawn into the circumference of the life of the soul.

The handle connects the subject to the vessel and serves as a further intermediary toward the spout, which, in turn, acts as an intermediary between the vessel and the world in the act of pouring out the contents. When we grasp the handle, "an entirely different life flows into the first" (that is, the inorganic is grafted onto the organic, like another life that is added to the animal life). The two "realms" interpenetrate, according to Simmel, because our soul "has its home in two worlds": the interior world, which also includes the body, and the world of external things. The soul itself achieves its fulfillment when—not in spite of, but thanks to the form that things impose upon it—it becomes almost "an arm which one of the worlds—whether the real or the ideal—stretches out so that it may seize the other."[62] Its prehensile nature in grasping the world, adapting itself to it, and the world flowing back into it, molding it through the senses, have their symbol in the handle of the vessel.

Bloch rediscovered the signs of history and of popular traditions in Franconia stoneware jugs shaped like a bearded man; his passion for collecting these Bartmann jugs (also known as Bellarmine jugs)[63] led him to trace in them the persistence of diverse characteristic elements: the shape of the pitchers used by Roman legionnaires, later rendered in a "soldierly, and then Nordic, coarsened" form, the memory of the signs outside German taverns that often reproduce a wild-looking bearded man (a forgotten image of St. Onofrius, a hermit who let his hair and beard grow for decades), and the link with death caused by their presence in funerals.[64]

In his turn, Heidegger modified Husserl's analyses of the living world thanks, above all, to the results obtained by reflecting on the activity of artisans and artists. Using the philosophical-poetic "idea of remembrance," Heidegger unraveled, in an even more radical way than Husserl, the philosophy of the schematic opposition of subject and object (typical of the "age of images of the world" and of its "metaphysics"), in such a way that even that which is obvious, banal, and "close at hand" can begin to express itself differently.

Heidegger's analysis, although the latest of the three (the first version of his essay "The Thing" dates from 1951), is the most well known. For Heidegger, the jug is presented physically as a receptacle with a bottom, sides, and a spout. For technical-scientific thinking, which purports to grasp things before and better than every other experience, the jug is the result of the labor of a potter, and its void is full of air. This kind of attitude—which goes back to Plato, who privileged the production of objects based on an idea—amputates the understanding of an object; it impedes not only seeing that the void of the jug is a potential container for what can be poured and offered as a gesture of hospitality or sacrifice to the gods but also the perception in this act of the further convergence of relationships within nature:

> The spring stays on in the water of the gift. In the spring the rock dwells, and in the rock dwells the dark slumber of the earth, which receives the rain and the dew of the sky. In

the water of the spring dwells the marriage of the sky and the earth. It stays in the wine given by the fruit of the vine, the fruit in which the earth's nourishment and sky's sun are betrothed to one another.[65]

Enveloped as they are in a symbolic patina that cannot be reduced to mere technical or logical aspects, objects absorb both natural relationships as well as social relationships, such as hospitality or religious gestures—for example, ceremonial libations.

If one disregards the forced stylization of Heidegger's *Geviert* (the "quartering" of heaven and earth, immortals and mortals), his often irritating jargon ("thingness," and similar expressions), and his labored attempt to find the "truth" of things, one can agree with Cippolletta's observation that "for Heidegger things do not exist in isolation—for example, a jug as a container for holding wine does not exist without the wine, or rather without the possibility of the wine, and therefore it is not independent of the wine, either; and it is certainly resting on a shelf, which is attached to the green wall, to the gilded mirror, to the dark window."[66] By grafting the lacerated connective tissue of a single object onto the world in all its complexity, our "idea of remembrance" opens up a chink in the direction of overcoming that "oblivion of being" to which the metaphysics of "the epoch of the image of the world" seems to have condemned mankind up to now, causing us to forget the fact that every entity belongs to the total horizon of senses into which it is inserted.

Heidegger's criticism of Husserl's phenomenology returns frequently to the accusation that in spite of everything Husserl's approach continued to maintain the separation between subject and object, since Husserl considered objects to be "simple presences" that are close to hand (the German term *Vorhandenheit* corresponds to the Aristotelian *ta prokeira*, which in the *Metaphysics*[67] indicates the first things that present themselves "under the hands" of those who contemplate the world with wonder).

Unlike Husserl, Heidegger treated objects as entities that demand something of us as human beings, that are before us (*Zuhandenheit*, "readiness to hand"), that confront us with their presence (*Dasein*). Heidegger believed that man must "take care of" objects without limiting himself to contemplating them in an exclusively theoretical way; above all, he must consider their "utilizability," the fact that they are a tool (*Zeug*) with a purpose. From Heidegger's perspective, objects "open up" to us in a primary practical-productive way that does not content itself with their simple presence. In the human environment, "hammer, tongs, needle refer in themselves to that of which they are made, that is, to steel, iron, bronze, stone, wood." Nature takes on meaning for man only when it is in a practical relationship to him: "The forest is a forest of timber, the mountain is a quarry of rock, the river is water power, the wind is 'wind in the sails.'"[68] Thus an object does not exist in and of itself, independent of its usability: "it is not given in the impression of the senses; its objectivity cannot be perceived by the senses, but only in the way in which we understand it within a world in which it is possible to use it."[69]

In one of his substantially autobiographical writings, "The Fieldpath," Heidegger recalled how, as a boy, he gave meaning and function to the oak tree that his father had chopped down in the forest:

> From the oak's bark, however, the boys cut out their ships which, equipped with rudder and tiller, floated in the Metten brook or in the school well. . . . Meanwhile, the hardness and scent of the oakwood began to speak more distinctly of the slowness and steadiness with which the tree grows. The oak itself said that "In such growth alone is grounded that which

lasts and fructifies." Growing means: to open oneself to the expanse of the heavens as one takes root in the darkness of the earth; that everything genuine thrives only when man is both in right measure: ready for the claim of the highest heavens and elevated in the protection of the bearing earth.[70]

Like works of art,[71] albeit with less power and fewer implications, objects trigger in those who use or contemplate them a series of references that flow from them as from a single, inextinguishable fountain of meaning. But the references that irradiate from objects do not proceed in a straight line, like rays of light, nor do they unfold in a concatenation of evidence, like the demonstration of a theorem. Rather, they come, as in a musical score, where the thematic nucleus and the variations on that theme do not unfold in a simple sequence of punctual instants destined to destroy each other—instead, they occur as a vibration, an oscillation, an expansion and contraction,[72] a wandering that enriches with meaning both the person who fantasizes and the thing about which he or she is fantasizing.

Unlike a thing, an object has no aura, no perception of appearing in a single form at a distance, as close as it may be:

To follow with the eye—while resting on a summer afternoon—a mountain range on the horizon or a branch that casts its shadow on the beholder is to breathe the aura of those mountains, of that branch.[73]

For Heidegger, too, when it is authentic, nearness approaches distance precisely because it is distant; it retains distance. But in our times, the trend toward eliminating distances in space and time doesn't bring us closer to things:

Man now reaches overnight, by plane, places which formerly took weeks and months of travel. He now receives instant information, by radio, of events which he formerly learned about only years later, if at all. . . . Yet the frantic abolition of all distances brings no nearness; for nearness does not consist in shortness of distance. What is least remote from us in point of distance, by virtue of its picture on film or its sound on radio, can remain far from us. What is incalculably far from us in point of distance can be near to us. Short distance itself is not nearness.[74]

With the elimination of long distances (and today, we might add, with the network of connections provided by satellite telephones and the Internet, which makes the origin or destination of a message a matter of indifference), everything becomes equally and chaotically near and far, because false nearness does not succeed in reconstructing an order for things.

Heidegger somewhat emphatically reached the point where he compared the merging of everything in the absence of distance to the explosion of an atomic bomb, which pulverizes and dissolves every object, blaming science for this annihilation (or masking of the "thingness of the thing"): "Is not this merging of everything into the distanceless more unearthly than everything bursting apart?"

More soberly, Walter Benjamin saw in the cancellation of the *hic et nunc* that is inherent in works of art the loss of an object's authenticity:

The authenticity of a thing is the quintessence of all that is transmissible in it from its origin on, ranging from its physical duration to the historical testimony relating to it. Since the historical testimony is founded on the physical duration, the former too is jeopardized by reproduction, in which the physical duration plays no part. And what is really jeopardized when the historical testimony is affected is the authority of the object, the weight it derives from tradition.[75]

In the perspective that I have chosen, the aura is, instead, the perception of the elusiveness and the additional characteristics of the thing that discloses its contents, conveying them in increasing measure to those who consider it but remaining inexhaustible in its depths.

2

OPENING UP TO THE WORLD

Deciphering the Inert

We are surrounded by an innumerable variety of objects that saturate our daily existence and are waiting to be understood, depending upon where our interests lie. These objects have diverse physiognomies, and each one demands that it be considered singly, according to a special sort of Linnaean taxonomy:

> In the form of technological objects, of consumer goods, of personal effects, of household furnishings and items, of the street and the city, or in the more ambiguous guise of artistic objects or marginal, obsolete presences, objects proliferate out of all proportion in every aspect of our life. Products are exchanged, consumed in increasingly large quantities and to an unprecedented global extent; they become an integral part of the identities of individuals and communities. They incorporate memories, expectations, feelings, and passions, suffering and the desire for happiness.[1]

We also have multiple relationships with things, inserted as we are in a peculiar web of relationships with and investments in objects, which contribute to giving consistency to our identity. We are constituted by means of things, and we are situated within the same horizon in which they are situated. From this point of view, "Kant, more correctly than Descartes, was to maintain that *ego* is more dependent on the object than viceversa."[2] And in fact, this is how Kant puts it:

> The desired proof must therefore demonstrate that we have experience of external things, and not mere fancies. For this purpose, we must prove that our *internal* and, to *Descartes*, indubitable experience is itself possible only under the previous assumption of *external* experience.[3]

Obviously, the human individual does not coincide with the objects that surround him or her or to which he or she is attached, and his or her identity does not depend, strictly speaking, upon things (nor upon the nonvital parts of his or her body). Personal identity and consciousness do not disappear, even if a "little finger" is cut off of the entire organism.[4] Also for Husserl, the ego escapes any objectivization, but things are part of it, like a horizon to be transcended, precisely because the intentional consciousness cannot disregard them.

The process of understanding the life of things can be compared, initially, to the process of someone writing a text, pouring his ideas, experiences, and feelings into it. Like Dilthey, we call the subjectivity of the writer "subjective spirit," and the text is "objective spirit," a transposition of signs onto a material support, representing what the individual thinks, imagines, feels.

Everything that surrounds us and that makes up the human world is the work of billions of people (the dead and the living) who have shaped reality, leaving traces that survive their work and their physical disappearance. To understand this world made by humans it is necessary—in a second moment—to behave like the potential reader of that text, retranslating into one's own language and inserting into one's own mental horizon the meaning and content that have been deposited in the text by the writer. Thus we rise from the "objective spirit" to a new "subjective spirit" of the person who interprets a text written by someone else. The person who interprets a text becomes intersubjective, when anyone who has found or deciphered a particular document decides to make public whatever had remained encased, in inert, dead form, within the objects that bore it: tombstones, monuments, papyri, scrolls, papers. Signs that had long remained indifferent or incomprehensible are then susceptible to becoming the patrimony of humankind, virtually available to everyone (one thinks of the deciphering of the Rosetta Stone by Jean-François Champollion or the unraveling of Linear B, the syllabic script used for writing Mycenaean Greek, by Michael Ventris and John Chadwick).

The passage from the objective spirit to the re-created subjective (or intersubjective) spirit restores and reelaborates that which other human beings had left behind them. We are virtually in a position to know all of the products of the human spirit because, according to Vico, *verum ipsum factum*, "this world of nations has certainly been made by men, and its guise must therefore be found within the modifications of our own human mind."[5] In the materials that they have left us—the traces of human thought—there remains, however, something that has not been produced by our species, even if we have manipulated it: stone, clay, metal, the fibers of papyrus, wood—elements that come from the foundation of nature and that, like our own bodies, have not been "made."

The "objective spirit" does not necessarily constitute a unique, hidden writing that is waiting *ab aeterno* to be discovered and interpreted. It is also a palimpsest, continually erased and rewritten, superimposing new texts over the old ones, which continue to show through. On the other hand, the objective spirit can be associated with the category of "social objects" that are recorded not only on paper and digital media but also in the memory of at least two people, as is the case with promises or verbal agreements. Maurizio Ferraris, referring to common episodes of daily life such as ordering a beer, offers an example of these social objects and their tacit, ramified implications in codified rules:

> Searle enters a café, and pronounces a French sentence: "Un démi, Munich, à pression, s'il vous plaît." Searle makes us notice that this very simple sentence triggers a huge invisible ontology: the social exchange between him and the waiter, a lattice of norms, prices, fares, rules, passports and nationalities, a universe of such a complexity that it would have had Kant shivering, if only Kant had thought about it. We are the postmoderns' antipodes. If postmoderns dissolve tables and seats by reducing them to interpretations, Searle's ontology asserts that also things such as promises and bets, shares and debts, medieval knights and Californian professors, tenures and symphonies possess a peculiar reality.[6]

The problem of materiality, of the shape and consistency of objects in the purview of the "objective spirit," was usefully complicated by the recent "analytic ontology" (a mere nod suffices here) that has begun to question, with rigor and subtlety, issues relating to the permanence of objects in diverse spatial or temporal contexts. Is the vase in a shop the same when it has been taken home? Is the vase of the morning the same one in the evening? How do we distinguish the materiality of the clay from the movements of the potter who gives it shape?[7] Seemingly, these are futile problems of popular metaphysics. Nevertheless, when examined closely, they have relevant implications in bringing us closer to a more articulated understanding of our relationships with objects and with the language that designates them. In an indirect way, these kinds of problems make us reflect on nature, on history, and on the way that specific materials are treated—as, in this case, how the clay is treated by the potter.[8]

The more we are able to integrate the objective spirit within our horizon of meaning, the wider our world becomes, taking on a greater profundity. If we possess the necessary information, specialized education, and adequate sensibility, everything becomes potentially significant and interpretable.

> Every square planted with trees, every room in which chairs are arranged, is understandable to us from childhood because human tendencies to set goals, produce order, and define values in common have assigned a place to every square and every object in the room.[9]

The arrangement of plants in a park or of furniture in a house, or the shape of an object formed by human labor, are laden with history, with meanings that can be reconstructed. And it is this, I would add, that distinguishes human beings from other animals:

> ... animals have no "*world*-space." A dog, for instance, may have lived for years in a garden and may have frequently been at all spots in it; but the dog has no complete overview of the garden with its arrangements of trees and bushes, independent of the location of its own body, no matter how large or small the garden may be.[10]

The transformation of objects into things (which also includes them becoming symbols, as occurs with an arrow or a cross),[11] also presupposes a developed ability to reawaken memories, recreate environments, get people to tell stories, and practice both "closed nostalgia," which turns in upon itself in regretting what has been lost, as well as "open nostalgia," which is capable of positively elaborating the mourning of loss, sewing up the wounds that are implacably inflicted on each of us by existence, enabling us to look forward.[12] In open nostalgia, things are no longer subjected to the unsatisfiable desire to return to an unrecoverable past—they do not adhere to the dream of changing the irreversibility of time, of overturning or perpetuating the sequence of events that occur a single time for all eternity, but that have become the vehicles of a voyage of discovery of a past laden with future possibilities.

The Duration of Things

The greatest danger is that not only things but history itself can be reduced to a great degree to a simple petrified objectivity, an accumulation of data and objects that are not illuminated by the deciphering and contextualization of their meaning. How will new generations be able to understand the messages left in things by preceding generations, saving them from the shipwreck of oblivion or from a fate of insignificance? How will they be able to connect them, with the appropriate mediations, to their own events and their own sensibility? For several decades, "material culture" has paved its own autonomous path in the realm of historical research, where it has attained its own place and its own dignity.[13] Material culture has ceased to be a minor genre, also because understanding the life of things requires just as much acumen as understanding the life of people, whether on a historiographic or a theoretical level. The *summa divisio* of Roman law between *res* (thing) and *persona* (person)[14] loses relevance in the realm of material culture since, when it is separated from its owners, the *res* maintains and transmits the traces of the meanings that had been attributed to it.

Nevertheless, it seems to many people that meanings and memories are incorporated less and less into the perishable objects that surround us, which are designed not to last long and can easily be replaced. The production of multiples—which goes back at least to the time of Roman sarcophagi—has often reduced the quality and, in the modern world, the durability of things, preventing their more stable placement in the framework of meaning:

> One of the fundamental characteristics of objects, once upon a time, was their permanence, the fact that they lasted. . . . Then just the opposite occurred—we began to live longer than our objects, which die before we do, not because of deterioration, because now we could make them last forever; they die because they become obsolete. In fact, they don't die: they function very well; they simply are replaced by other, more advanced objects.[15]

Thus the assertion contained in the penultimate line of Borges' poem "*Las cosas*" becomes problematic: "They will endure beyond our vanishings."

On a cosmic level, based on the regular cyclical movement of the celestial bodies, Augustine had identified a *magna rerum constantia* in the disorder of sensible material.[16] But Augustine knew, as did Lucretius—albeit from the Christian perspective of the relative brevity of what is created—that in the sublunar world that is subject to corruption, even the most durable things, which have survived several human generations, eventually wear out:

> Again when passing years have come and gone,
> The ring upon your finger grows quite thin
> By constant use, and dropping wears the stone,
> The crooked share of iron smaller grows

Although you see it not, within the fields;
The flints upon the streets worn by the tread
Of multitudes decay, and by the gates
The brazen statues show their hands grown thin
By touch of men, when passing to and fro.
Thus all these things grow less when rubbed away:
But when the various particles depart,
This jealous Nature will not let us see.[17]

With the development of technology, there come into play objects that are different from those that we are accustomed to see around us—objects that are made of materials that have come out of "the depths of stone, of wood, of clay, of iron."[18] Unless one is a specialist, who today is able to recognize many of the approximately six million products derived from petroleum, none of which originally existed in nature? Their source—hydrocarbon, which takes a million years to form—is destined to be exhausted in a relatively short time, but the remains of their use, like that of certain minerals, will last longer than we would wish—things like plastic bags, the lead and mercury that have been dumped into our rivers, and other substances such as the radioactive waste from nuclear power plants.

It is said that, in order to survive, consumer society must destroy things that last. There is no longer a slow disappearance but rather a "violent loss" of objects; the taste for acquiring things and "shopping" constitute the premise for this work of destruction of what has been purchased.[19]

Discarded objects and materials, however, are not always destroyed. They may be given a new function and recycled. In industrialized nations, fabrics are made from used plastic bottles; in some African populations, aluminum cans that had contained beverages from the Western world become bracelets or toys; and in the Italy of the second postwar period, inner tubes from old tires were used as life preservers for swimmers.

The case of a village in the interior of Sardinia, Bitti, is noteworthy, particularly in the sheepfolds in the surrounding countryside. In this village, local things, made to last and produced from imported materials that are transformed *in loco*, were progressively replaced over the course of the twentieth century by "things that come from outside," *cosas istranzas*, already made for use and no longer produced according to traditional methods and forms.

> In the traditional village-space, few objects came from the world outside. No food products were brought in except salt, preserves, and sugar. Everything relating to clothing, household furnishings, or iron, copper, or leather goods arrived in the village in its raw form. What arrived from outside was not objects, but materials that were transformed into objects by the tinsmith, the iron-monger, the tailor, and the cobbler.[20]

This is why *cosas istranzas* did not carry any precise message:

> The process through which an object acquires meaning is born of the relationship and by the agreement between shepherd and artisan, and takes place within the rural community. In addition, the raw material that comes from the outside world must fit into the list of an inventory that has already been culturally established by usage, by the demands, and by the affectivity of the work of the peasant; for whom, for example, the fabric should necessarily be velvet or moleskin, and of a specific pre-selected color.[21]

Today in the village, as in the sheepfolds, objects arrive from the outside world already made because it is cheaper to buy them than to have them made to order by a local tailor, cobbler, or potter. Once their contents have been used up or have achieved their function, they are repurposed: "a tin of Saiwa biscuits" is filled "with nails, pliers, hammer, hacksaw," and a plastic colander is put to unique new uses. Something similar takes place today in American Indian tribes on the Pacific coast between the United States and Canada, where the potlatch—the ritual ceremony in which the participants complete with one another in giving prestigious gifts to demonstrate their rank and humble the other competitors—now includes the use of objects such as plastic baskets, used as containers for the gifts, something that would have been unthinkable in the past.[22] The distance between objects like this and the jug considered by Simmel, Bloch, and Heidegger couldn't be greater.

In our world, it is inevitable that the panorama of objects should change rapidly, that a "generation" of constantly new or fashionable models should take the place of and push the preceding models into oblivion. More elaborate computers quickly render obsolete computers manufactured a few years earlier; electric ovens or microwaves take the place of the traditional hearth where logs burned and the spit was turned by hand. If technologies, demands, and tastes change, why should we remain attached to the things and technologies of the past? Why follow, in a snobbish way, the fashion of antiques and place in beautiful displays— without understanding them, as simple trophies of wealth and presumed distinction—objects that will never have an intrinsic relationship with us and that have not been adopted out of "love"? Yet precisely because they reestablish the connections between the various segments of our individual and collective history, to save things from insignificance means to understand ourselves better.

How long things last does not depend solely on spontaneous natural processes. In history, we frequently find a sense of pleasure generated by the destruction of things, a voluptuousness that does not look toward a possible reuse of objects but aims rather at their demise, in material as well as symbolic terms. This is the case with vandalism, in its apparent gratuitousness; of sacked cities that are destroyed and burned during times of war; of rage that vents itself upon objects; of *jacqueries* and popular rebellions.

Popular revolts, in particular, dictated by the confused desire to obliterate the hated symbols of a particular regime, at times turn into actual revolutions, as in the storming of the Bastille in Paris in 1789 or the Bolshevik attack on the Winter Palace in Saint Petersburg in 1917.

> The crowd particularly likes destroying houses and objects: breakable objects like window panes, mirrors, pictures and crockery; and people tend to think that it is the fragility of these objects which stimulates the destructiveness of the crowd. It is true that the noise of destruction adds to its satisfaction; the banging of windows and the crashing of glass are the robust sounds of fresh life, the cries of something newborn. It is easy to evoke them and that increases their popularity. Everything shouts together; the din is the applause of objects. . . . But it would be wrong to suppose that the ease with which things can be broken is the decisive factor in the situation. Sculptures of solid stone have been mutilated beyond recognition.[23]

In the triangular relationship between the individual, the masses, and the object, the pleasure of destroying is linked to the firm decision to negate the limits imposed by the ruling powers, limits on the bursting energy with which the masses feel momentarily invested and on the freedom to which they tumultuously aspire.

The concept of *damnatio memoriae*—as exemplified by the erasure of inscriptions, decapitating of statues, burning of books or of entire libraries, iconoclasm, the "vertical" oblivion pursued by

Christians in building churches on the sites of pagan temples—clearly shows the close connection between the pleasure of destroying and the desire to wipe out names, symbols, and places by means of a violent affirmation of a new power, fed initially by hostility, the thirst for revenge, the desire for redress, fanaticism, and envy of that which is deprived of prestige with a view to establishing new hierarchies between people and between people and things.

To Fill a Void?

Meanings can be taken away from or added to things, but they can also be infused with value to an excessive degree, almost as if to overcompensate for other losses, similar to what happens in the Freudian "work of mourning." What have we lost in our civilization and in our lives to make us focus with such ardor on merchandise? What void do consumer products fill? Is it really true that in societies dominated by the market and by "possessive individualism," in which the economic sphere has become relatively autonomous, our relationship with the world of things has taken on a higher meaning than that between humans?[24] Are we so conditioned by merchandise that it occupies the first place in our interests? If the sense of ownership or attachment to objects has always existed, albeit with different modalities, what is it today that differentiates our relationship with the things that we make our own? What distinguishes a figure like Mastro Don Gesualdo[25] from one of our own contemporaries who is obsessed by shopping?

It is not easy to grasp the phenomenon of consumerism in its multiple facets without divesting oneself of the veil of moralism. In philosophical terms, a more advantageous point of view from which to examine the issue of consumerism is by considering it to be, from the time of its genesis, a result of the abolition of the limitations on the full satisfaction of long-repressed needs and desires that had traditionally been imposed by penury.

Since 1852, when Aristide Boucicault opened Au Bon Marché, the first department store in Paris (the store still exists today, in the Rue de Sèvres), the world has been marked by the preeminent role of consumerism in the economy, in society, and in the psychology of the individual. Low prices, the possibility under certain conditions to return things that have been purchased, and the ability to make payments over time have triggered successive waves of "the proliferation of the superfluous" and "the democratization of luxury."

Several innovations that have become familiar to us have further contributed to the volume of material goods that can now be purchased: fifty years after the birth of the department store, customers were enticed to explore these huge stores by show windows, invented in 1902 by a Belgian engineer named Émile Foucault, who developed a process for producing large panes of glass that could withstand drastic changes in temperature; in the 1930s, the American businessman and inventor Sylvan Nathan Goldman, by creating the supermarket shopping cart, encouraged customers to fill them with merchandise—much more than what the baskets that had been used previously could hold.[26]

From a theoretical point of view, the department store emerged as a result of the impulse of French economists, pupils of Frédéric Bastiat, who wanted to reduce the gap—identified by Simonde de Sismondi in his *New Principles of Political Economy* of 1817—between the overproduction of merchandise caused by the massive introduction of machines and underconsumption, attributable to the low buying power of a large part of the population. The basic premise of these economists was that making it easier to purchase merchandise would succeed not only in absorbing the surplus of goods produced but also in reducing the levels of unemployment in industry and commerce and in preventing unemployed workers from destroying the machines that they held responsible for their loss of work. In our lifestyle, however, there is something more than just the removal of obstacles to acquiring goods that—beginning in the 1920s—rapidly spread first in the United States and later in other countries and continents. Our age is characterized by a sort of acquisitive bulimia, an excessive inclination to satisfy needs and demands that are substantially superfluous. The relative abundance of merchandise has led individuals to break down the millennia-old barriers imposed by scarcity—provoking, according to some critics, a disturbing regression of civilization to a primitive state: "Objects are neither a flora nor a fauna. And yet they do indeed give the impression of a proliferating vegetation, a jungle in which the new wild man of modern times has difficulty recovering the reflexes of civilization."[27]

Given the fact that objects participate directly in the construction of individuality, this regression seems to contribute to a serious loss of people's authenticity; in our present-day affluent societies, people are seen as incapable of overcoming their own desire to embrace the world of objects (an attitude that is not always an indication of passivity but often of a close adherence to the functioning of an economic system based on the need to consume). In this way, the impulse of individuals to educate themselves for the better would be extinguished: "There is no transcendence any more, no finality, no objective: what characterizes this society is the absence of 'reflection,' of a perspective on itself."[28] If this were true, a paradox would be triggered: the loss of what is real along with the incapacity to raise oneself above it, and the upward impulse that had characterized European humanism—from the treatise *On the Sublime* by the Pseudo-

Longino to the Renaissance tradition, and from the seventeenth century until the middle of the twentieth century—would be completely devoid of energy and motivation today.[29]

If we accept the notion that consumerism overall produces nefarious effects, can we and should we break away from it? Given the fact that in our economic structure if there is no consumption there is no production, and if there is no production the system fails, it is evident that consumption is inseparable from the entire economic cycle. For this reason, although the current financial and energy crises will perhaps change some collective behaviors, the elimination of practices linked to consumerism—which is also the consumption of life, and not only of goods—would be long and arduous. It would implicate the weakening and, at worst, the destruction of the current mode of production, as well as the painful reconversion of hundreds of millions of people from lifestyles to which they had for not very long, and with evident pleasure, become accustomed.

That is at the social level. At the individual level, does the consumption of merchandise beyond what is strictly necessary for the satisfaction of primary needs imply, in and of itself, an arid loss of reality and a radical banalization of one's existence, an existence deprived of the power to transcend and renew itself? Not everything leads us to accept such catastrophic scenarios. The invitation of Viscount Georges d'Avenel to remember that modern luxury is indeed banal but that before modern times there was nothing banal but poverty retains its validity today. And it is worth remembering that there are "zones of resistance, niches, secondary routes" in which objects resist becoming merchandise and become symbols that are not necessarily based on advertising—symbols that "reveal their capacity to orient our behaviors" in the most personal way.[30] Broadening the range of the satisfaction of needs beyond the most necessary products does not automatically imply the end of transcendence, with the consequent regression of humankind to a savage state in a jungle of objects. From certain perspectives, in fact, it represents the appreciable result of a laborious process of civilization that involves innumerable people and continues to be affirmed after millennia of forced, humiliating abstinence from material and immaterial consumption. Does there exist, on the other hand, an inexorable destiny that obliges us to accept the permanence of an economic system based on wasting resources precisely when more than a third of humanity suffers from an excruciating lack of basic goods? Can this relative luxury, distributed in an asymmetrical manner among the various populations and within each of them, continue to last for long without becoming an intolerable injustice? What will happen when the wealthiest countries will, perhaps, be forced to share their goods with the inhabitants of other parts of the globe, previously condemned to endemic scarcity? Will we really return to long-forgotten ways of living that are more sober and frugal, and as a result will our relationship with merchandise, objects, and things change? And if such changes should actually take place, what desires, ideas, or fantasies will we project onto things? Will we rediscover, in different forms, what the opulence of many has up to now pushed to the margins of our awareness—the origin of things in nature, in history, in technology? Mindful of Keynes's warning that "the inevitable never happens. It is the unexpected always,"[31] it would be reckless to formulate any prediction for the medium and long term; the questions remain open.

The Epoch of Banal Things

Do we effectively live in the epoch of the multiplication of "banal things"? The impression is widespread and tenacious: "Our culture treats as commonplace the object and its role in society. It forgets the place and function of the object, or else wishes to see in it only the expression and means of our utter alienation."[32] Things are reduced either to pure materiality or just the opposite: simulacra and standard-bearers of signs, mere instruments of communication.

Have we ended up losing sight of the labor necessary to produce merchandise, reducing it to aggregates of symbols? Has the perception of merchandise as the crystallization of labor, the fruit of ingenuity, of the toil and often the exploitation of countless men, women, and children gotten to the point that we have forgotten that work transforms not only that to which it applies but also the person who works? Considered over the long duration of time, has work really gone from being the result of a biblical curse— the expiation of the sin committed by Adam and Eve in the Garden of Eden—to a Calvinistic sign of salvation, and from an emblem of dignity and of the "self-emancipation of humankind" to a painful or tedious tool for survival?

The lottery of nature has distributed the gifts of the earth— fertile land, drinking water, climate, metals, sources of energy, ease of communication, locations in the major currents of traffic—in a random manner with respect to the populations of our planet. Thus both populations and individuals have always fought for control of resources (it suffices to observe the configuration of borders between nations to realize how they essentially depend on wars): while the more fortunate have received these gifts directly from nature or have appropriated them by force, the less fortunate do not have access to them, or only in a very limited way (as is often the case of people who live in inhospitable places, or of nations devoid of political or military power or that do not yet possess the technologies and culture necessary to utilize adequately their own resources). Has the eclipse of the value of labor contributed to the transformation of merchandise into simulacra, so that behind the façade of a brand name—which *should* be a guarantee of quality—products invite us to live in an ethical and political dimension that is "protected by signs and in negation of reality?"

Is it completely true that "Now, we know that the Object is nothing and that behind it stands the tangled void of human relations, the negative imprint of the immense mobilization of productive and social forces which have become reified in it"?[33] Although this diagnosis contains a massive dose of the rhetoric of postmodernity—"it is certain that the status of things in the postmodern world has changed, but to go so far as to say that things no longer exist is taking quite a leap"[34]—it is evident that the value of the use and exchange of objects today has partially given way to their transformation into simulacra or their exhibition as mere status symbols.

Since the time that, in certain countries and on certain social levels, consumerism surpassed production and waste surpassed saving, mere possession of the goods necessary for existence, even in abundance, is no longer considered satisfactory. Thus many people are led to consume and make a show of symbols, to choose fashionable icons that distinguish them from other people and that, at the same time, place them within certain social categories. In the realm of this logic are born the "myths of today," which focus on cult objects such as the Citröen DS of the 1950s or the recent Smart Cars, or designer handbags and accessories.[35]

Mass production, which creates replicas that are indistinguishable from an original that doesn't exist, but also the diffusion of images—both those torn from the *hic et nunc* of the real space and time of film, from television, from the Internet or from cell phones, or those created by artificial reality and by virtual reality—all contribute to the conception of objects as simulacra.[36] Virtual reality, in particular, not only bypasses direct contact with objects; it also succeeds in mimicking the sense of touch, which, like the sense of sight and the sense of hearing, makes the same experience reciprocally sharable by multiple individuals. By means of visors placed in special helmets and sensors attached to the wrists, different individuals, following the same computer program and coordinating among themselves, can simultaneously receive the sensation of touching the same immaterial objects.

Feelings of Guilt

Faced with the accumulation of acquired objects whose purchasers get rid of them quickly, many people in the Western world are assailed by feelings of guilt because of their excessive consumption of merchandise and feel a sense of disgust for their crass display of that merchandise. Thus the desire to "liberate our life of excess fat" is periodically triggered—a weak resolution that serves to alleviate our guilty conscience for just a few moments. More effective, from the consumer's perspective, is the objective of constructing "an intelligible universe with the goods he chooses,"[37] conceived as part of material culture and integrating factors of his own identity into that universe. The recent trend in sociology and economics is, for that matter, to downplay the negative effects of consumerism, to no longer consider, for example, the customer as a passive, heterodirected individual, a victim of advertising, but rather as an active subject who, with his own choices, assigns value to the world in which he lives.[38]

In reality, excessive acquisition and consumption of merchandise seem often to obey the adaptation of many people to the criterion of making a virtue of necessity, to the obscure awareness that their ideals of happiness pass through the Caudine Forks of socially admitted and permitted and even pleasant pathways, rather than free choices. In his novel *Les choses*, Georges Perec has shown that the price of the small, momentary doses of happiness that we manage to grasp by adhering to the dominant values of the consumer society is the impoverishment and superficiality of human relationships, as happens to his protagonists Jérôme and Silvie, once they have attained the state of well-being to which they had long aspired.[39] Paradoxically, the exaltation of merchandise as a vehicle of happiness brings with it a devaluation of that very merchandise because it makes it functional not for the effective motivations of individual people but for an extrinsic social order, the "cultivation of 'taste,' aimed, however, no longer at the revelation of an individuality, but rather at the communication of the social stratum of those to whom it belongs."[40]

The competition to conform to social models of real or presumed excellence has always existed, and Simmel has discussed this extensively with regard to fashion[41]—a fleeting phenomenon, in its "mysterious banality," because it does not correspond to exigencies of beauty, utility, or comfort.[42] Fashion's efficacy depends upon the interweaving of two paradoxes. The first is temporal in nature because time reveals itself both in the act of devouring and disqualifying its own phases the moment they have passed, as well as in its own capacity to regenerate itself, to be constantly reborn and renewed. The second paradox is social in nature because everyone wants to be original, even though they end up being just like everyone else (on account of the growing imitation of a model that urges those who wish to distinguish themselves on to further innovations, setting in motion an indefatigable dialectic). On the basis of the first paradox, fashion prevails over that which endures and that to which an intrinsic significance is attributed. On the basis of the second paradox, individuals believe that they are preserving their own identity through imitation: they want to signal that they belong to a particular group without completely identifying with it. The pretense of authenticity intersects with artifice, and sincerity mingles with simulation and dissimulation. Fashion simultaneously conceals and reveals the individual, who has become opaque to himself: "Known unto these, and to myself disguised," Shakespeare has one of the characters in *The Comedy of Errors* say.[43] In its scope, revelation has the dual meaning of disclosing individuals to themselves and concealing them again beneath a veil, inserting them into a social game of reciprocal seduction (etymologically, attracting them to themselves: *ad se ducere*).

Household Gods

One wonders whether a noble sort of nostalgia for preindustrial civilization, vaguely reminiscent of Pasolini—nostalgia for a time when penury was linked to a "transcendence" also of a religious nature and when peasant culture was linked to handmade objects—will rise up against the culture of merchandise and mass-produced objects. Will we regret the world of yesteryear, where the few things that people acquired by dint of sacrifice, carefully preserved and handed down, would slowly absorb cognitive and emotional investments, thus becoming conceptually richer, emotionally more charged, and materially better constructed?

For a deeper understanding of the reasons for nostalgia for the (presumed) authenticity of the things of past times and the consequent aversion for the "pseudo-things" of the present, an exceptional document is the letter from Rainer Maria Rilke to Witold Hulewisz, written from Rilke's retreat in Muzot, Switzerland, on November 13, 1925:

Even for our grandparents a "house," a "well," a familiar tower, their very clothes, their coat: were infinitely more, infinitely more intimate, almost everything a vessel in which they found the human and added to the store of the human. Now, from America, empty, indifferent things are pouring across, sham things, dummy life. . . . A home, in the American sense, an American apple or a grapevine over there, has nothing in common with the house, the fruit, the grape into which went the hopes and reflections of our forefathers. . . . Live things, things lived and conscient of us, are running out and can no longer be replaced. We are perhaps the last still to have known such things. On us rests the responsibility not alone of preserving their memory (that would be little and unreliable), but their human and laral value. ("Laral" in the sense of the household gods.)[44]

A similar attitude with respect to the "history of ordinary things" can also be found in more recent authors such as Roche, who dedicated his book to "those who suffered from the chilblains of winter, who could not read at leisure because the power was cut off or petrol hard to find."[45] The laral atmosphere of the home nurtured and facilitated the transformation of objects into things and, with its sacral intimacy, bestowed decorum and respectability on the owners of those things. Even in preindustrial societies, objects and those who owned them bestowed a fundamental sense of importance precisely within the "oikonomic" sphere, centered on the home, before the term "economy" was broadened by the Italian philosopher Antonio Serra in 1613 to include not only the management of a home but also of society at large.[46] From Xenophon of Athens' *Oeconomicus*[47] to the "home as everything" of the European tradition (in which the home was considered a place of production as well as of consumption and services),[48] it was women who attended to domestic matters and, usually delegated to do so by their husbands, took care of the things that the family possessed and cultivated the pleasure of accumulating and organizing those things.

Until not so long ago, the home was above all the image of "petrified time"; it brought together and condensed "the past and the future in the inhabited space which was built in the past and modified by successive generations."[49] Evidence of this are the household furnishings in Roman homes of the seventeenth century, where wealth was represented by precious objects and jewelry, often received as part of a bride's dowry or as testamentary bequests—things that were "tendentiously inalienable" and protected by the law but also subject to a series of successive reappropriations via inheritance and custom.

Even in the humblest social strata, the plethora of furniture, kitchen equipment, and furnishings is not considered as a simple ensemble of functional tools. In the selection and care of these objects, in keeping them shiny and ready to use, other criteria and values prevail, mostly centered on the tastes of women. "This apparent contradiction between greater poverty on the one hand and a greater accumulation of things on the other, is, in my opinion, a sign of a different attitude with regard to objects—not purely utilization, nor too closely related to the availability of money; I would define it as the particular pleasure of possessing household items, of surrounding oneself with them, caring for them." Not only in the accumulation of things like silverware and jewelry or in collecting paintings but also in increasing the number and variety of pots and pans there is a "sacrifice of the useful." For the poorest people, it is a sign of self-esteem; for the most well-to-do, it is a sign of social ascendency. "By being transformed into objects removed from the sphere of usefulness and simply put on display, those resources of time and money have not been uselessly immobilized, in unproductive enterprises; rather, they have created value, of a different and higher type than economic value, capable of conferring prestige during one's life and permanence after death."[50]

As always, material things transmit immaterial symbols—in this case, personal and social values. For that matter, the imagination is normally inclined to attribute an emotional meaning to the home, which is considered almost archetypically as a shell of intimacy and "the first world of the human being," the custodian of "memories of stone" and wood, from the walls of the home to the wardrobe or the bed.[51]

In the domestic sphere, objects are mediators between people in another way as well. For example, for a long time the notion of patrimony used to be decisive for arranging marriages. Parents, relatives, or guardians decided whether a couple would marry based on considerations of a substantially economic nature or in view of family and political alliances—a custom that has remained in what is left of the European monarchies and aristocracies and that is still reflected in the Spanish language, where the son-in-law is called *hijo político* (political son) and the brother-in-law is called *hermano político* (political brother).

Starting with Rousseau's *New Heloise* and the novels of his English contemporaries such as Richardson in *Clarissa*, the choice of a spouse was decided, instead, based on the wishes of willing individuals. There is in this attitude the tacit application to human relationships of a sort of Newtonian law of attraction that, not without risks, is made to take precedence over considerations of an economic or social nature. In marriage, the ideal of love became more important than that of patrimony, and the woman ceased to be virtually a simple pawn exchanged between families.

The choice of the person to marry is a more recent conquest than the selection of furniture, fabrics, or paintings, which in the homes of the well-to-do in the preindustrial age were ordered on commission, in accordance with the personal taste and prestige of the owners of the home. Today, the custom of commissioning specific objects from craftsmen or artists has become costly and rare, also because people are practically constrained to choose mass-produced objects even when it comes to luxury items—which, thanks to worldwide networks of production and marketing and an expositive system that is permanently governed by the visibility of advertising, can now be found everywhere.

With regard to traditional "bourgeois" furnishing, in which, "diversified with respect to function, the furniture is highly integrated, centering around the sideboard or the bed in the middle of the room," occupying, in their monumental imposingness, the center of the domestic space, the modern object—also on account of the lesser availability of living space—tends to recede, losing its specific function: "Corner divans and beds, coffee tables, shelving—a plethora of new elements are now supplanting the traditional range of furniture. The organization of space changes, too, as beds become day-beds and sideboards and wardrobes give way to built-in storage. Things fold and unfold, are concealed, appear only when needed." The advantage of such a way of organizing living space is reflected in the greater freedom of the individual to organize the space in which he or she lives and in an ambiguous liberalization of the functionality of objects that does not, however, liberate them from their "fruition."[52] What remains to be understood is how it is possible to emancipate oneself from the fruition of these objects, without sleeping on the bare earth or devouring food raw, standing up and eating with one's hands.

The Inflation of Beauty

An object produced by craftsmanship, characterized by technical mastery, by the desire to carry out conscientiously one's work and by the obsession with "quality-driven" results, at times reaches levels of excellence that annul the distinction between an object of craftsmanship and an art object, as in the case of the famous saltcellar of Benvenuto Cellini or the violins of Antonio Stradivarius.[53]

Any object that is commissioned and created as a unique exemplar is certainly more susceptible to being charged with meaning and emotion. But in the end, doesn't the same thing occur with mass-produced objects that are designed by highly specialized groups of people according to prototypes that are elaborated with great care and taste? And even if they don't reach great heights of quality, doesn't one's own automobile or, to an even greater extent, a doll purchased for a little girl in an ordinary shop also take on the character of an *unicum*—don't they become inseparable from the individuals who live with them?

Today, beauty has burst through its barriers—it has emerged from its splendid isolation in churches, palaces, and museums and has flowed into the streets and the objects of everyday life. Linked to functionality as an additional value, beauty has been transferred to automobiles, shop signs, armchairs, coffee makers. The prevailing esthetic certainly produces "inflated beauty,"[54] but through the art of design and the use of new techniques and materials, it often guarantees quality as well.

Objects today generally become things not so much because of the cognitive and emotional investments that people make in them (which might come later) but rather because of the effect of advertising, which surrounds them in a gleaming aureole that is often capable of distracting one's gaze from the intrinsic trustworthiness of the product. Acting as an artificial accelerator of consumerism, advertising projects phantasmic qualities onto merchandise, which nevertheless remains anchored to the tastes and archetypes that most captivate a particular audience: youth, health, beauty, security, pleasure, happiness, family, tradition, adventure or innovation, and, above all, eros.

Advertising has become an art capable of manipulating symbols and calibrating them according to the target audience and the prevailing fashions of the moment, but it is naïve to imagine absolute spontaneity and authenticity in the consumer's choices. In any period of human history, there have always existed admen and merchants interested in selling their products through a panoply of expedients. In a "toy-driven" economy like ours, which is regulated by the interests and inclinations of consumers (because it can no longer impose its merchandise on consumers, as in the heyday of Henry Ford with the Model T), advertising is even more indispensible for synchronizing consumption with production, in terms of both quantity and quality.

This is one of the factors that favors the ascendency of the "sex appeal of the inorganic," an expression that emerged to indicate the attraction of fashion as an "motley cadaver," a dead shell that covers a living body,[55] but that today designates the assumption on the part of the object of an erotic component so strong as to capture the subject that experiences its fascination and transform that subject into a "feeling thing."[56] With a power of attraction analogous to that exerted by the Latin concept of *venustas* (a word that denotes loveliness or charm, deriving from *Venus*) the object, enveloped in fabricated dreams, attributes to the subject an ephemeral identity, a façade. Not only does it affect human sensibility (*aisthesis*); also, pushing the subject aside, it makes it more dependent on the thing. In addition, by producing addiction, it deprives what is beautiful of its aura—its dazzling, moving, unique appearance. Paradoxically, it ends up by nonestheticizing the subject. Once "the cultural responsibility" of one's choices is taken away, the only thing left for the subject is to "attempt to respond to the solely cultural desire for the thing, establishing with it an alliance that is sensual rather than spiritual, emotional rather than logical."[57] Even if objects are impregnated, in a different way and at a different speed, with symbolic values, and even if there exist appreciable points of equilibrium between form and function—on some rare occasions it is the form itself that obliges the constructors of an object to change its function[58]—the logo, the *griffe*, the global recognizability of a brand or of a design tends to prevail over the quality of the object itself.[59] As an effect of research, materials undergo an incessant process of improvement (more rapidly than in the past, when, for example, the improvement of the composition of metal used for knife blades during the sixteenth century made it possible to produce scalpels and other surgical instruments that were less painful for patients than the barber's razors that had been used up to that time, or when, in 1668, the glass factory at Saint-Gobain succeeded in producing large-scale mirrors).[60] In our own time, suffice it to mention the development of lightweight wool for summer clothing and athletic wear or the use of nanotechnologies to produce materials in the field of precision mechanics.

Although they are not capable of restoring the aura of uniqueness to objects, "places of quality" continue to exist, and, in conferring their consistent quotas of added value, today they are situated at the crossroads between thought, art, and technology. They have been summarily individuated (other than in the "school of the philosopher" and, I would add, in the industry supported by so-called product designers) in the artisan's workshop, in the scientist's laboratory, and in the mechanic's garage.[61] These are places where elements of a technical, economic, or cultural nature that had previously been isolated become coagulated and meld together, giving rise to a new object that will last as long as the environment in which it operates continues to exist. This phenomenon is called a "lash-up."[62]

Beauty and functionality are interwoven in another way as well. Thanks to biotechnologies and artificial intelligence, today we are witnessing a "bioconvergence" between the organic and the nonorganic, the natural and the artificial. Through the use of prostheses (from the simplest such as pacemakers or low-invasive coronary bypass operations, to the most complex, such as microchips that restore sight to the blind), our bodies are being filled with devices made of metal, silicon, or plastic that improve both our health and the way we look; on the other hand, in computers, which are increasingly affected by design, human intelligence is minimized and the use of nanocircuits is posited for the elaboration and transmission of data. We are moving toward the so-called *posthuman*— the increasingly tight integration of living material and inert material, between new forms and new contents.[63]

A "fourth realm" of objects is born, and it becomes possible to imagine objects "no longer as prosthetic instruments, extensions of the body and of the mind, but as 'others' from us, like partner-instruments. They increasingly resemble autonomous organisms, and the world of objects increasingly resembles a fourth realm, alongside the realms of animals, vegetables, and minerals."[64] Fortunately, this fourth realm does not fear the extinction of species and the consequent diminution of biodiversity.

The work, intelligence, imagination, and emotion absorbed by products need to be deciphered (an undertaking that becomes all the more difficult the further away one gets from their original time and culture). Beyond any regret for the past and for the dimension of the house conceived as protected by tutelary deities, beyond any resentment for the "Americanization of the world" and its utilitarian model of dealing with things, there remains a serious preoccupation that was pointed out by Dilthey: the worry that our relationship with the "objective spirit" can become opaque and unintelligible, that we run the risk of wandering in a jungle of symbols that are not understood and things that are destined to remain orphaned or dead. Dilthey's fear was, in fact, that people would end up losing the meaning of the messages of the past and that the historical experience would therefore tend to become impoverished or indecipherable, infecting the present with the same ills.

Fortunately, the deposits of the "objective spirit," which would seem to be simple fossils, are not inert: they remain active, even if they are on the edge of the sphere of awareness, where they exert an unperceived influence. We become aware of them, in an indirect way, because they "gravitationally" affect the trajectory of the individual's way of being, thinking, and feeling (as when, in the field of astronomy, the mass of an unknown planet disrupts the orbit of a known planet). Thus if we can succeed in making them enter into the span of attention of a subject, the latent layers of meaning of the "objective spirit" become the material with which the object can enhance itself.

It is the constant, conscious intervention of individuals, marked by the energy and "warmth" of their activity and their efforts at interpretation, that prevents the objective spirit from becoming blocked, frozen in incomprehensibility. This intervention is now all the more urgent because the members of the most developed contemporary societies—unlike their forefathers, who had been integrated into more stable, cohesive communities—are no longer able to presuppose a "world of life" that is relatively lasting and shared, a "tacit dimension" in which they can put their faith.[65]

The Art That Saves

The strategies for giving or restoring meaning to things follow diverse doctrines and cultural traditions. I will list of few of them here, simply to indicate their diffusion on a worldwide scale. Think of the Chinese wise man "with no ideas" who renounces any preconceived hierarchical viewpoint and takes into consideration the equal admissibility of everything,[66] or the Japanese, who have developed a veritable veneration for teacups and who, on the occasion of the elaborate ceremony of drinking tea, exclusively use objects "characterized by the quality of *wabi-sabi*, which indicates poverty and essentiality, but also the capacity to express past time that has already been lived."[67] Returning to European philosophy but taking into account its assonances with Japanese Zen Buddhism, how could we not recall the attitude of serene abandon, of relaxed flowing of thoughts and sensations, *Gelassenheit*, as a state of mind propitious for the emergence of a relationship with things that is not limited to them simply being close at hand?[68]

Among all these pathways, the most promising seems to be that of art, down which contemporary philosophy has ventured as a privileged itinerary toward restoring to things those meanings that have been eroded because they were considered superfluous or marginal; meanings that have been eroded by the usury of habit, by the loosening of historical memory, and by the practice of scientific generalization.

Art is precisely what introduces us to what is nearest to our heart—a special kind of *pragma*, *cosa*, *res*, *Sache*—that is, the inexhaustible nucleus of meaning of things, from which emerge the human labor, intelligence, and creativity that were locked inside the individuality of each work of art. Unlike mathematics, physics, logic, or "philosophy as a rigorous science," in the case of art it is not the *auto to pragma* or the *Sache selbst* that speaks and evolves *more geometrico* in a single, necessary direction; rather, it is the meaning and symbols that branch out in various directions to then thicken, coagulate, and focalize themselves in forms that can be incessantly elaborated. To compensate for the loss of "secondary qualities" decreed by modern physics and by Cartesian thought, a part of the philosophy of the twentieth century therefore attempted to comprehend the excess meaning that things absorb in the field of art and of daily experience. As demonstrated in Descartes' famous description of wax in his *Meditations*, qualities that can be perceived by the senses evaporate, and only what the mind can grasp remains. In Descartes' philosophy, and in the classical physics of objects, there remains only the *res extensa*, the quantitative space, neutral and homogeneous, the only thing that the *res cogitans* can know according to the criteria of the "new science." As Merleau-Ponty writes,

> . . . at the base of an objective ontology, there is the conviction that the work of the philosopher, reflecting on Being, consists in bringing about a purification of the immediate contact that we have with Being, in such a way as to discern what is solid, what resists understanding. Exterior nature is then reduced, according to Descartes, to extension.[69]

Although it is quite well known, it is worth rereading this excerpt from Descartes' *Meditations*:

> Let us take, for example, this piece of wax. It has just been taken from the honeycomb; it has not yet quite lost the taste of the honey; it retains some of the scent of the flowers from which it was gathered. Its colour, shape and size are plain to see; it is hard, and can be handled without difficulty; rap it with your knuckle; it makes a sound. In short, it has everything which

appears necessary to enable a body to be known as distinctly as possible.[70]

Initially, therefore, the object's secondary qualities are revealed, involving and impregnating all of the senses. Later, however, the piece of wax undergoes a metamorphosis that cancels out those qualities:

> But even as I speak, I put the wax by the fire, and look: the residual taste is eliminated, the smell goes away, the colour changes, the shape is lost, the size increases, it becomes liquid and hot; you can hardly touch it, and if you strike it, it no longer makes a sound . . . the wax was not after all the sweetness of the honey, or the fragrance of the flowers, or the whiteness, or the shape, or the sound, but was rather a body which presented itself to me in these various forms a little while ago, but which now exhibits different ones.[71]

What remains? "Certainly nothing remains excepting a certain extended thing which is flexible and movable." Everything is reduced to an extension, to what can be grasped only through "purely mental scrutiny [*solius mentis inspectio*]; and this can be imperfect and confused, as it was before, or clear and distinct as it is now, depending on how carefully I concentrate on what the wax consists in."[72]

Although the duality of *res cogitans* and *res extensa* was destined to end with the philosophy of Spinoza, where thought and extension constitute the two attributes of substance (different but complimentary perspectives for regarding the same totality of nature), this Cartesian duality introduced a theoretical wedge that would divide European culture for a quarter of a millennium, almost up to the threshold of the twentieth century. During this entire period, qualities of sense were, often implicitly, either abandoned to esthetics, to the qualitative dimension of beauty as perceived by the senses (no longer linked to truth and goodness as in the age-old metaphysical trinity),[73] or reduced in contemporary terms to the *qualia*, the qualitative states of the psychological experience of the individual. Qualities of sense are thus transformed from scientific knowledge to art and from objectivity to the sphere of mere subjectivity.

Polemicizing in a sometimes sterile manner against science and technology (and ignoring, even after its publication in 1958, the fundamental work of Gilbert Simondon about technical objects as mediators between nature and man),[74] contemporary philosophy has attempted to recuperate the wealth of qualities and meanings that things can absorb or transmit, restoring to them, on a theoretical level, the depth that literature, art, or historiography had normally already bestowed upon them. It was clearly realized that bringing things back to the universality of the concept necessarily involves the impoverishment of experience, almost as if to compensate for the undeniable advantages that are obtained in this way through the knowledge of nature.

By establishing an alliance, art and philosophy have carried out an act of opposition against the impoverishment of experience. In this way, philosophy has been induced to concede greater space to the imagination or, rather, to make better use of that faculty that includes both art and philosophy, which Kant called "reflective judgment" and which Hannah Arendt took up also in the form of political judgment. When, for example, we see a shantytown, we begin to concatenate and intertwine a series of reasonings, hypotheses, states of mind, and images. We reflect, for example, on the nature of poverty, on the deprivation and sacrifices to which poverty constrains millions of people, or on the injustice of a particular social order. Our mind follows several possible lines of thought, gradually focusing on one or another aspect of experience suggested by the vision of the miserable shacks and their inhabitants. Then we use judgment as the "mysterious endowment of the mind by which the general, always a mental construction, and the particular, always given to sense experience, are brought together."[75]

Something analogous occurs in our relationship with things, especially in the realm of art. Following the example of art, philosophy has been called upon to comprehend the transformation of objects into things, to restore to them the additional meaning that has been taken away by the usury of habit and by the objectifying view. Thus both art and philosophy combat the desemanticization to which our daily life has been subjected, being reduced to a "desert of the real." At the same time, art and philosophy are an invitation to rediscover in things the aura that brings them closer to us while still maintaining a certain distance.[76]

It is now possible to conceive of the realm of artistic fantasy as an atopia, an unclassifiable place, irreducible to the space of the *res extensa*, which belongs neither to the realm of absolute reality nor to its polar opposite, the realm of utopia, of nonexistence by definition. It is an unlocatable zone in which both cognitive and affective desire find their most intense fulfillment (at least for the limited time of the "Sunday of life" in which Hegel encased the enjoyment of art, removing it from the working days of the week and the worries of day-to-day existence). In this zone there is manifested the paradoxical near distance represented by the "unknown fatherland" of which Plotinus and Novalis speak, or that *arrière-pays* glimpsed by Yves Bonnefoy—a symbolic space where we have never been but that seems to us as if we have always known it, almost as if it were a foreign country inside of us—lost, and at times briefly rediscovered: "I have in mind a phrase of Plotinus—regarding the One, but I'm no longer sure where it comes from, or if I'm citing it correctly: 'No one would walk there as on foreign soil.'"[77]

Should we say—like the painter-soldier Michel Kraus in Pierre Mac Orlans' 1927 novel *Quai des brumes (Port of Shadows)*—"I paint the things hidden behind things," or repeat, with Jaufré Rudel, that "My heart has no joy of any love / Except that of him who has never lived"? Or, with Goethe, recognize that "*Was ich besitze, seh ich wie im Weiten / Und was verschwand, wird mir zu Wirklichkeiten*" ("All that I have stands off from me afar, / And all I lost is real, my guiding-star")?[78] Or should we take to their ultimate point the implications of the paradox expressed by Giorgio Caproni?

I returned there
where I had never been.
Nothing, from how it was not, has changed.
On the table (the checkered
cloth), half-filled
I found the glass
never filled. Everything
is still as
I have never left it.[79]

What we have never lived and to which we nevertheless aspire is the world of desire in its unappeasable and paradoxical near distance or distant nearness: it is what we try in vain to grasp in its fullness and totality, what we most long to understand and grasp emotionally, the *quaestio* that it would be urgent to discuss but that always escapes us and is manifested only through allusions.

We experience a similar state of mind—quite common, albeit enigmatic—when we leave a place that is known to us:

Everyone knows that feeling of having forgotten something in one's waking life that didn't come along and become clear. That's why it often seems so important—something one had just wanted to say, but it slipped one's mind. Leaving a room where one has lived for a longer time, one looks about strangely. Here, too, something stayed back that one was never able to find. One takes it along nonetheless, and starts with it again somewhere else.[80]

There are many other situations in which we seem to be on the verge of understanding the messages that emanate from things without, in the end, succeeding in grasping them. The goal eludes us, leaving behind it the anxiety and uneasiness of an unkept promise, the sense of the depths of an unfathomable world that is also the echo of our own depths. As in a puzzle, the messages that things emit with their Baudelairean *confuses paroles* seem to awaken latent, enigmatic nuclei of meaning that are so beyond us as to inhibit their full comprehension by the subject that experiences them. They are, in fact, too close to the source of thought, to the depths of the imagination, to the tumult of the passions from which they flow and from which concepts, images, and feelings branch out.

What has eluded us? What remains? The sensation of an unsaturated experience, like many others, but particularly the impression that the meaning of the important events of our life remains attached to things, to places. This sensation is also linked to the ingenuous questions that children (or adults, in moments of idleness) ask about how things appear when we are not there. Childhood fantasies about objects that come alive during the night—when, while humans sleep, the objects are left alone—recur frequently in fairy tales. In "The Steadfast Tin Soldier," Hans Christian Andersen tells a story about how objects come alive during the night:

> Now the toys began to play among themselves at visits, and battles, and at giving balls. The tin soldiers rattled about in their box, for they wanted to play too, but they could not get the lid open. The nutcracker turned somersaults, and the slate pencil squeaked out jokes on the slate.[81]

The animated film *Toy Story*[82] depicts a group of toys that come down from their shelves and discuss the possibility that some of them will eventually be thrown away by the boy to whom they belong. Some authors have perceived in the subtle suspicion of an "animation of the inorganic" "man's uneasiness with regard to the objects that he himself has reduced to 'the appearance of things.'"[83] But on a positive note, we should add that it is also a matter of man's effort to restore to objects that which the dominance of the values of usefulness and exchange had taken away from them.

The Underside of Things

In its reflection on art and, in particular, on individual works of art, twentieth-century philosophy reopened the dialogue between things and people. Heidegger was the much-discussed protagonist of this dialogue in his famous analysis of Van Gogh's painting of a peasant woman's shoes.[84] In the painting, the shoes have lost their function. They no longer serve their everyday purpose; they are no longer a simple object that is close to hand, ready to be used. Rather, they communicate a nucleus of meanings—disclosed each time we regard the visual work and intimately connected to their depiction therein—meanings that are released only thanks to the removal of the object from the immediacy of its simple presence. Heidegger demonstrates this in a highly imaginative prose style:

> In the stiffly rugged heaviness of the shoes there is the accumulated tenacity of her slow trudge through the far-spreading and ever-uniform furrows of the field swept by a raw wind. On the leather lie the dampness and richness of the soil. Under the soles stretches the loneliness of the field-path as evening falls. In the shoes vibrates the silent call of the earth, its quiet gift of the ripening grain and its unexplained self-refusal in the fallow desolation of the wintry field. This equipment is pervaded by uncomplaining worry as to the certainty of bread, the wordless joy of having once more withstood want, the trembling before the impending childbed and shivering at the surrounding menace of death. This equipment belongs to *earth*, and it is protected in the *world* of the peasant woman. From out of this protected belonging the equipment itself rises to its resting-within-itself.[85]

In reality, the painting depicts Van Gogh's own shoes, not those of a peasant woman—it is the case of "an object experienced by the artist as an important part of himself, an object in which the painter observes himself as in a mirror."[86] Yet despite the fact that Heidegger misinterpreted this painting, it is certain that in works of art things appear in a new light, imbued with cognitive and affective meanings that are not included in their value as objects for use or exchange. *Res ipsa loquitur*, as used to happen in an eminent way in the classical Greek world—sculptural and architectural works by the great masters "*spoke for themselves*. They spoke, that is, they showed wherein the human belonged, they allowed one to perceive whence the human would receive his determination."[87]

In the realm of the phenomenological tradition, Maurice Merleau-Ponty has, in his turn, shown in an exemplary way how painting is capable of guiding thought to "ground itself upon things themselves,"[88] thus restoring to them that plurality of meanings that naturalistic reductivism had erased. Merleau-Ponty explained how painting metaphorically makes us intuit both the invisible in the visible as well as—to use an expression of Ernst Bloch—"the underside of things," what is glimpsed beyond their surface:

> In front it's bright, or brightly lit, but no one yet knows wherein the *dark side* of things consists that we alone see, let alone their *underside*, and what it all floats in. We know only the front or right side of their technical subservience, their benign incorporation; no one knows whether their (often preserved) idyll, temptation, natural beauty is what it promises, or pretends to hold.[89]

A painter can see the world in a more articulated and profound way than those who have never exercised and refined that gaze that in all of us "envelops, palpates, espouses visible things." A similar perception, "as though it were in a relation of pre-established harmony with them, as though it knew them before knowing them," constructs situations in which things themselves seem to speak and to regard us, to the point that we no longer know who is seeing and what is being seen: "so that finally one cannot say if it is the look or if it is the things that command."[90] In educated perception and in painting, things pass into us, and we pass into them, because their *connaissance*—knowledge—is a *con-naissance*—a joint birth of subject and object. Cézanne, for example, was capable of bringing forth things from the opacity of everyday perception, of letting things express themselves without placing himself in opposition to them—causing them, in fact, almost to be born, to blossom before our eyes as happened when he fulfilled his lifelong desire to paint "a white tablecloth like a layer of freshly fallen snow, on which the silverware stands out symmetrically, crowned by blond rolls."[91] Technically, Cézanne succeeds in doing this by following "the swelling of the object in modulated colors" and by indicating "*several* outlines in blue. Rebounding among these, one's glance captures a shape that emerges from among them all, just as it does in perception."[92]

My body is part of the world, but:

> Visible and mobile, my body is a thing among things; it is caught in the fabric of the world, and its cohesion is that of a thing. But because it moves itself and sees, it holds things in a circle around itself. Things are an annex or prolongation of itself; they are incrusted in its flesh, they are part of its full definition; the world is made of the same stuff as the body. This way of turning things around [*ces renversements*], these antinomies are different ways of saying that vision happens among, or is caught in, things . . . in that place where there persists, like the mother water in crystal, the individedness [*l'indivision*] of the sensing and the sensed.[93]

In perception, activity and passivity coincide, and this, I would add, is how the object can express itself.

3

LIVING NATURE

To Love Things

An excellent example of how art not only maintains the secondary qualities of objects but also transforms them into things is found in still-life painting,[1] particularly in seventeenth-century Netherlandish art.[2]

In the art of the seventeenth-century Netherlandish masters, mimetic and illusionistic realism is extreme and refined, but it does not exhaust the meaning of the painting. Beneath their material covering of canvas, wood panel, images, and colors, the things depicted in these paintings conceal precise and encoded symbolic values—and, by their very nature, symbols connect what is visibly represented to what is invisibly absent; thus grapes allude to the blood of Christ or oysters to sexual pleasure.

The vegetables, fruits and cut flowers, game, fish, and shellfish in these pictures are all things painted for the pleasure and enjoyment of people. They appear suspended between their ephemeral or recently extinguished life and their death, between their solid visible form and the evanescent perspective of their imminent dissipation or decomposition. They testify at one and the same time to the pleasures of life and the desire to take advantage of those pleasures before it is too late, to the fulfillment of all five senses and their progressive weakening, to happy moments and their passing, and to the usefulness and beauty of everyday goods and their transitory nature. Baroque painting often emphasizes the transitory nature of things with the presence of objects such as a skull or a soap bubble, the emblem of the *homo bulla* (the metaphor of man as a bubble), or with the depiction of short-lived insects or small animals such as flies, dragonflies, butterflies, moths, grasshoppers, or millipedes.

The term *stilleven* originated in Holland and appeared for the first time in inventories drawn up around 1650. In 1675, the German artist and art historian Joachim von Sandrart used the expression *stillstehende Sachen*—things that are still or mute.[3] Initially this genre of paintings was called "rhopography," from the Greek word *rhopros*, meaning trifles or trivial things, a term translated by Vasari as "little things,"[4] but these things could also be described—borrowing the words of the librettists Illica and Giocosa of Puccini's *Madame Butterfly*—as "humble, silent little things."[5]

The earliest examples of this genre date back to the third century BCE; Roman wall paintings and mosaics offer abundant illustrations—see, for example, the *Bowl of Fruit* from Boscoreale, now in the Metropolitan Museum of Art in New York. In the modern age, the revival of still-life painting is attributed to two panel paintings by the German painter Ludger Tom Ring the Younger, *Bowls of Flowers*. In Italy, still-life painting became popular first in Lombardy, particularly with Caravaggio and Arcimboldo.[6] From Italy, this genre of painting began to spread throughout Europe; it flourished in the Netherlands soon after 1600, the date that separates its history from its so-called prehistory. It has been noted that the Netherlandish painters rendered the innovations and the ideas of the Italians "in a more directly, more sensually realistic manner."[7] Since then, still-life painting has known a lasting popularity that continues to the present day. Among the painters of still lifes of the twentieth century it is enough to think of Matisse, Picasso, De Chirico, Morandi, Warhol, or Lichtenstein.

Stilleven literally means immobile (or silent) nature, and it depicts a group of things selected and taken as themes by a painter, who separates them from contexts that originally included the presence of human beings—typical objects are those that traditionally appeared in paintings depicting Saint Jerome or Saint Augustine. The object thus becomes the subject or protagonist of the painting and comes to be admired for itself, it becomes autonomous, it turns into something that we care about; it is no longer what is in front of us as an obstacle to be overcome or an otherness to be incorporated. We no longer need to subjugate the object, precisely because art itself has removed it from immediate consumption and the struggle to obtain it. Objects, transformed into things, obviously do not have any language as such; they do not respond to our questions with words. They initially appear inert and do not seem to reciprocate our ideal, symbolic, and emotional investments. But if we observe them carefully, forsaking our ignorance of them, they make us speak on their behalf and lead us toward their progressive self-revelation—or to use, in a different context, the title of a book by René Girard—objects make us pay attention to the "unheard voice of reality."[8]

Using the French preposition *entre*—which has a double meaning ("within" and "between") that is lacking in Italian or English—we could say that whoever looks at a painting is projected "within" or "inside" the work while simultaneously maintaining the distance "between" himself and the work. The viewer contemplates the painting in its stillness, its silent speech, and its disturbingly exclusive self-reference, which, nevertheless, still demands the viewer's involvement. The sight of what is represented in the painting is, in a Kantian sense, "disinterested," but in reference to the Latin *inter-esse*, "being in between," it establishes a relationship of reciprocal implication. In this regard, we are deeply "interested" in what sets us free either from the habit of dealing with objects as conceptually, symbolically, and emotionally insignificant or from the prejudice that detached contemplation, deprived of any involvement, is the supreme degree of knowledge.

Painting goes beyond the pure reproduction of objects; it simultaneously represents something more and something less than their physical nature. By transfiguring the object, art achieves a paradoxical enhancement of reality. It recreates reality while depriving it of its solid consistency. It enables us to enter another dimension, removed from the picture frame, the "door to the world," inventing enclaves of extraterritoriality and extratemporality embedded in ordinary time and space. *Stilleven* slowly defeats the prejudice that once considered it to be a "minor genre," far removed from history, mythology, and sacred images. Still-life painting excludes men, who boast of superior dignity, and depicts not only ordinary "small things" but also luxury goods such as porcelain, crystal vases, or elaborate saltcellars. But it is the images of humble objects that help us rediscover the wonders of everyday life.

It is like a meditation on the words of Plotinus: "We wonder at the novelty, but we should wonder at the customary and at our everyday experiences;"[9] it is like remembering Heraclitus's dictum that "there are gods even in the kitchen;"[10] it is as if Nietzsche's invitation to "become good neighbors of the nearest things"[11] had been accepted in advance; it is like making an effort to look at ordinary things from unusual points of view;[12] or, finally, alluding to the title of a now famous book, it is as if alongside the gods of great things, "the gods of small things" were also taken into account.[13] *Stilleven*, "intended for private enjoyment,"[14] moved paintings from solemn settings such as churches, courts, or palaces into the homes of merchants, bankers, ship owners, jurists, or doctors, whose portraits simultaneously reveal both the trials and the joys of life.[15] One of the reasons for this dislocation is that, in the Calvinist Netherlands, artists could no longer engage in painting sacred subjects to be displayed in churches, which were now bare and had no ornaments beyond music and singing and commentary upon verses from the Bible. In the Netherlands at that time, there was a shift from triumphalist paintings that publicly celebrated the glories of religion or politics to a style of painting with fewer pretensions, collected and hung in the intimacy of private homes.

The domestic dimension and the expression of attachment to the things of the world and its comforts—which was not a sin for the hard-working Calvinists but rather an indirect sign of divine benevolence—was associated with the praise of prosperity and the apotheosis of abundance. During its golden age, with fewer than two million inhabitants, the Netherlands was the wealthiest country in Europe.[16]

A great variety of goods arrived at the ports of the Netherlands from the most remote corners of the world thanks to a *sui generis* form of globalization, created by the East India Company and the West India Company, which formed a wide network of commerce covering half the planet—from Indonesia to the Caribbean, from Formosa to Brazil, from Tasmania to Novaya Zemlya, from the present-day Ghana to Suriname—and based on financial investments that involved a significant portion of the population, ready to risk their own money in commerce and navigation.

Therefore the things depicted in *stilleven* can be seen as symbols of the goods and the commerce that brought the world to the

Netherlands and the Netherlands to the world. The variety and quality of merchandise resulted from the import of products such as grains, citrus fruits, wine, iron, copper, furs, rugs, tobacco, tea, pepper, and other spices, and from the export of butter, cheese, herring, porcelain, and books.[17] Flowers—which had been particularly appreciated during the previous pictorial tradition—took on an important economic role in the Low Countries, as highlighted by the speculation on tulips that between 1634 and 1637 gave rise to the phenomenon of "tulipomania."

Although sometimes these paintings go hand in hand with a symbolic exhortation to moderation and frugality, they usually depict images of abundance and auspices of future prosperity. In the Netherlands of the seventeenth century, the allegory of opulence—in the form of the satisfaction of basic needs for food and drink, with the implicit praise of the victory over hunger and thirst—was frequently portrayed in images of markets, kitchens, and butcher shops, where quartered oxen and swine, poultry and game, fish and shellfish, fruits, jugs, and glasses of wine or beer make a beautiful display. Here the poverty of the peasant Simulus in Virgil's *Moretum*, which I quoted at the beginning of this book, is openly defeated; it is exorcised by the abundance and assortment of good things to eat and drink.

Stilleven in the golden age of the Netherlands was expressed in diverse typologies and subclasses—in the case of food, all linked to daily life and the rhythm of fairs and festivities: the simple breakfast (*ontbijtije*), the ordinary midday meal (*middageten*), the *banket* or public feast, the snack, the more or less abundant light meal, or the sumptuously decked table. The most frequently represented style was the ornate *pronkstilleven* or "luxury still life," distinguished by its complex compositions and splendid colors. As an allusion to other pleasures and other senses besides taste, there are depictions of floral compositions, pipes and smoking equipment, musical instruments, and books. Finally, there are representations of *stilleven* paintings themselves in the form of pictures hung on the walls of homes, such as in the *Interior with Jacket on a Chair* by Cornelis Bisschop, now at the Gemäldegalerie in Berlin, where a still-life painting depicting a huge lobster and some wine glasses on a table hangs on the wall.

In *stilleven* things are represented at their *toppunt*, a Dutch expression that means the point of perfect maturity, when things fully display their qualities—when they are at their zenith, before their inevitable corruption. Things participate in the common destiny of everything that is born and dies; however, painting gives them durability—it secures them in their mute persistence. Their temporary nature is redeemed, and their enjoyment—promised by their immediate consumption in the form of food, drink, smoking, music, or reading—becomes practically endless for the eyes of any possible future consumer. Things are exalted, or "blessed" as Ortega y Gasset said, referring to the paintings of Rembrandt, where they shine in their ordinariness with an almost supernatural light:

> It often happens in the pictures of Rembrandt that a humble white or grey cloth, a coarse household utensil, is found wrapped in a luminous and radiant atmosphere, with which other painters surround only the heads of saints. It is as if he said to us in gentle admonition: *Blessed be things!* Love them, love them.[18]

To bless things means—not only in Rembrandt—to defy the *contemptus mundi* (contempt for the world) that casts them into caducity and insignificance, liberating them, symbolically, from the curse of the ephemeral. This is how art, compared to science, "saves phenomena" in their individuality, reintroduces meaning and secondary qualities, making every fleeting moment fulfilling by removing it from the relentless succession of time and, as far as possible, from the cycle of generation and corruption. In this way, the primacy of the philosophy of *respice finem* ("look to the outcome"), the tendency mournfully to project the present into a future of annihilation, is negated. Instead, the present is captured in its full splendor, in the plenitude of its own manifestation.

In pictorial representations—and later in photography and film—things are transposed to another space, suspended in time, and protected from oblivion, decay, and death. Furthermore, in portraits, the gaze of the subject depicted is linked to ours, drawing us beyond the painted surface. An explicit and moving example of this is a 1646 portrait in the Civic Museum of Cremona by the painter Luigi Miradori, known as Il Genovesino, which memorializes a dead child. The little boy, Sigismondo Ponzone, is shown standing; with his right hand he holds a large dog by the collar, and with his left hand he indicates to the viewer a scroll bearing the inscription:

> Father, you who
> participated in my creation
> take me now
> newly transformed
> by art.[19]

Between the Eternal and the Impermanent

In the Netherlands of the seventeenth century, there was a tacit effort to adapt men and women to the increased instability of social life and to the acceleration of historical time, but this effort took a different direction there than it did in the Baroque culture of Catholic countries such as Spain or Italy. In the Netherlands, there was no shortage of anxiety, given the uncertain political and military situation facing the country. Its citizens were exposed to an extraordinary series of challenges. Inside the country, tensions erupted between the partisans of the Stadtholder William of Orange and those of the Grand Pensionary Johan de Witt—both Johan and his brother Cornelis de Witt became victims of this internecine strife; they were assassinated and dismembered by the enraged mob in the *ramjaar*, "the disaster year" of 1672. In the international arena, in under a century the country endured the so-called Eighty Years' War, the Dutch war of independence against Spain that began in 1568 and officially ended in 1652; the war with England for the control of maritime traffic, between 1652 and 1672; and finally the war with France that began in June 1672 and ended with the Treaty of Nijmegen in 1678. That conflict had begun with a deliberate flooding of a large section of the country in order to halt the troops of Louis XIV of France.

These conflicts were not generally reflected in mournful images of death; instead, the anxiety of the Dutch population transformed itself into mute acceptance of danger and caducity. Precisely because these feelings were shared, they appeared less threatening to a country that had proudly carved out its lands from the sea. The enjoyment of worldly things not only came from the fact that Dutch Calvinism interpreted wealth as a sign of divine benevolence toward the saved—a benevolence that, in contrast with the Catholic perspective, was independent of good deeds and repentance—nor was it only connected to the wealth generated by the citizens in guilds and in different branches of the economy, but it was also connected to the general ethos, which opposed life to death and *toppunt* to *vanitas*.

For a variety of reasons, in Catholic Baroque art the function of instability and caducity was felt with more drama than in the Netherlands. For one thing, from the philosophical point of view, the notion of ontology—a term coined ironically in 1613—began to break up during this period. The notions of substance and essence began, in other words, to disintegrate, and, conversely, "modes" and "accidents," relationships and manners, became more relevant than the presumably immutable and intelligible core of entities.[20] That which was secondary, accessory, and contingent—which was not strictly necessary, since it could be or not be—now became a priority. At the same time, the symbolic aspect outstripped the material aspect of things; the way that people and things presented themselves imposed itself upon their intimate—and by this time presumed—"substance." And time manifested itself in its most insatiable voracity, in the act of consuming its barely elapsed phases rather than in its capacity for self-regeneration, for constantly being reborn anew.

The kind of work of art referred to as *vanitas* does not view objects *sub specie aeternitatis* ("under the aspect of eternity") but rather in their transitory nature. In *stilleven* painting, on the contrary, things become "miniatures of eternity"—to borrow an expression from Jeanne Hersch; they open a "gap in time" toward the absolute, which is touched fleetingly at the point of contact between becoming and eternity, thus hinting at what remains in that which passes away.[21] Attaining immobility and impassivity through art and detaching itself from the domain of becoming in which objects are necessarily destined to disappear, the ephemeral tends to become eternal in painting. The work of art helps resolve the apparent contradiction inherent in the expression "the life of things," because "life"—which refers to what is born and dies—remains in the things that are captured at a single moment in time in still-life paintings.

Dutch painting inherited—how consciously, I cannot tell—the traditional philosophical meaning of the term "eternity." We have forgotten this particular meaning, as we are used to think of eternity in the function of time and therefore to conceive of it as a very long, in fact infinite, time. However, neither the Greek word *aion* nor the Latin *aeternitas* has any relationship with the notion of duration (*aidiotes*). These words refer, first and foremost, to life and its fluids—such as seminal fluid, tears, or even the marrow of the spinal cord;[22] then, they refer to the duration of the life given to men by the gods; after that, to the very life of the gods;[23] and, finally, to the fullness of life in general. This last meaning appears in Plotinus, who defines *aion* as *zoe* or, more precisely, *zoe en stasei*, "life in a state of rest."[24]

Plotinus's definition was revised and clarified by Boethius, who called eternity *plenitudo vitae* (the fullness of life),[25] and it was further reformulated—in a variation that Borges was fond of evoking—by the nineteenth-century Lutheran bishop Hans Lassen Martensen: *Aeternitas est merum hodie, est immediata et lucida fruitio rerum infinitarum* (Eternity is merely today; it is the immediate and lucid fruition of an infinite number of things). Talking about eternity, Borges himself added:

> True, it is unconceivable, but then so is the humble successive time. To deny eternity, to suppose the vast annihilation of the years freighted with cities, rivers and jubilations, is not less incredible than to imagine their complete salvation. . . .[26] Life is too poor not to be immortal.[27]

Nevertheless, the conception of eternity given by Plotinus remains fundamental as the point without extension from which all life emanates: "total life, all together and full, absolutely unextended, that is inherent to the essence of Being."[28] It is the inexhaustible fountain that nourishes and preserves life, that gives and expands while remaining always identical to itself; it is the unitary energy that produces multiplicity (*hen-polla*, in opposition to the One, *hen-hen*). Indeed, the human soul is the nexus that unites time and eternity: it is able to rise toward the "unity-multiplicity" articulated in itself and to merge with the One, or to decay, to descend, to disperse in the contingent and the ephemeral. One might say that, in the metaphysics of Plotinus, the life of things represents the flow of multiplicity from the *aion*, which enjoys stability but is not stability per se:

> Eternity, therefore—while not the Substratum [not the essential foundation of the Divine Principle, the One, *hen*]—may be considered as the radiation of this Substratum: it exists as the announcement of the Identity in the Divine, of that state—of being thus and not otherwise—which characterizes what has no futurity but eternally is.[29]

In contrast, time is the moment of the generation and corruption of beings, their "paying the penalty"—in the words of Anaximander—by being removed from eternity, from the fullness of life, while trying to imitate it. Time is therefore a hemorrhage of life, a loss. Time is poverty (*egestas*, as Boethius would say), need, a useless race toward the unattainable fullness that is barely glimpsed.

Therefore, what is this *zoe en stasei*, this fullness of life in its *toppunt*, if not a still life removed from the transitory, impoverished dimension of time?

All the Faces of Rembrandt

It has been pointed out that seventeenth-century Netherlandish painting paid particular attention to individuality and to things captured in their unrepeatable nature—an idea that has been suggested in discussing a possible affinity between the paintings of Vermeer and the philosophy of Spinoza.[30] But early on, Georg Simmel had already argued vigorously for the primacy of individuality in Rembrandt's portraits and self-portraits. (Rembrandt rarely ventured into the genre of still life, but his *Still Life with Two Dead Peacocks and a Girl*, circa 1639, in the Rijksmuseum in Amsterdam, is one exemplar.)

According to the most recent research, during his lifetime Rembrandt completed more than a hundred self-portraits, recording, in a sort of illustrated diary, the progressive changes in his own appearance. For more than forty years—from the first image in which he portrayed himself, the *Stoning of Saint Steven* from 1625, to his last painting in 1669, the year of his death—Rembrandt depicted himself in a variety of expressions and costumes. One of the most representative of these self-portraits is an oil painting of 1629, preserved in the Alte Pinakothek in Munich, in which the young Rembrandt's face has almost to be guessed at under an enormous mop of artfully ruffled hair—arranged in huge curling bangs covering his eyes, which are nearly reduced to slits. There are also three etchings from 1630, at the Rembrandt House Museum in Amsterdam, where the painter appears with a glowering expression, eyes wide open, and an arrogant demeanor. And, finally, there are all the drawings, etchings, and paintings that depict Rembrandt dressed as a soldier, a beggar, a saint, an Asian, a nobleman with a gold chain and a fur coat or an embroidered shirt, or otherwise adorned with the most diverse types of headgear. Among the self-portraits from the time of Rembrandt's old age, between 1660 and 1669—a period marked by grief, poverty, and the pitiless ravages that time and the experience of sorrow wreaked on his face—the *Self-Portrait with Palette and Brushes* of 1662 at the Kenwood House in London and the *Self-Portrait with Hands Clasped* of 1669 at the National Gallery in London stand out.[31]

All of these paintings and etchings reveal a layering of different periods: a progressive accumulation of the past, setting the pace of existence for a man who knows he is doomed to the gradual corrosion of time and the ultimate triumph of death. With the intensity of his gaze in these works, Rembrandt puts the past back into play; he reveals its successive layers, and, at intervals, he exposes its presence. Giving spatial form to time, he transforms a sequential process into simultaneity, and extracting light, color, and the cycles of time from the darkest depths, he lets them fall in delicate waves on the shores of the visible.

No other painter has devoted so much time to the study of himself, particularly the changes that his face underwent. Everything in Rembrandt's face is significant, down to the smallest detail: from a wrinkle on the forehead to a thinning of the lips, from a contraction in the pupil to the blush of the cheeks. By its very nature, the human face has a depth that manifests itself on its own surface. Time and space coexist there: the furrows or the wrinkles that age, habits, and events have deposited there contain and tell a story. They constitute the precipitate of events and states of mind that have been transformed into character and facial features. In the face, the passing of time is crystallized in the space of compresence. In Rembrandt's self-portraits, the act of becoming is transformed into a motionless *res extensa* that nonetheless retains secondary qualities and symbolic values.

More than any other painter, Rembrandt showed in his self-portraits how the human face concentrates the maximum of time in the minimum of space to produce images that testify to its gradual deterioration. From one self-portrait to the next, he progressively accentuates the signs of the desecrating distance that the passage of time brings to the face. From this perspective, Rembrandt's paintings and prints can be considered documents of the manifold ways that an individual appears over time and also as surfaces where certain thoughts and passions can be interpreted in their manifestation or concealment. We are used to the cartography of the face because from childhood we have learned to decipher its features. But have we become similarly capable of reading the signs of time, the imperceptible variations that the passage of light, color, and form leave on things? Have we sufficiently experienced, for example at sunrise, the tiny mutations that light emerging from darkness confers upon things? Have we carefully observed the imperceptible or sudden change of color, or the rearrangement of images and shadows at different times of the day, as Monet did when he painted his famous series of haystacks? Have we captured the continuous variation in tone that the color of things undergoes by shifting our observation point in space? Have we ever been amazed and moved by these small metamorphoses, by the daily miracle of things becoming presences?

Simmel saw in the work of Rembrandt the reflection of a "Germanic" conception of "becoming"—though not in a racist sense, as in the popular book on Rembrandt from Simmel's time by Julius Langbehn[32]—in clear contrast to the classic Greek and Latin tradition, fully present in Italian Renaissance portraiture and based, according to him, on a static metaphysics of "being." If—as Simmel claimed, quoting Goethe—"life can only be thought of insofar as it flows,"[33] then its flow should not be trapped in rigid structures. According to a conventional and overly simplistic idea of the Italian Renaissance, the marmoreal solidity of Italian portraits seems to shatter only because of external causes. For Simmel, in many such portraits,

> One gets the impression that death would come to these people in the form of a dagger thrust. With Rembrandt portraits it is as if death were the steady further development of this flowing totality of life—like the current with which it flows into the sea, and not through violation by some new factor but only following its natural course from the beginning.[34]

By contrast, in the portraits from the Italian Renaissance the flow of becoming is frozen in timeless form, codified according to ideal types; individuality is lost, and facial features are emphasized rather than softened, precisely because the reference to universal models is solid.[35] The "factors of *becoming* are excluded. Like the steps of a calculation where only the result is of interest, they are of no concern." Rembrandt, instead, "transposes into the fixed uniqueness of the gaze all the movements of life that led up to it: the formal rhythm, mood, and coloring of fate, as it were, of the vital process."[36]

But Rembrandt's self-portraits not only depict an accumulation of the past; they also seem to be looking toward an unspecified and obscure future. In a letter to his brother Theo, dated October 1885, Vincent van Gogh noted, in reference to Rembrandt, that "*il faut être mort plusieurs fois pour peindre ainsi*" ("one must have died several times in order to be able to paint like that").[37] Especially during the last phase of his artistic production, Rembrandt expressed in his self-portraits the increasing weight of caducity, the ineluctable encounter that everyone will have with death—a path on which he had been preceded by younger people who were dearest to him, such as his first wife Saskia, his second wife Hendrickje, and his son Titus. In this respect, his late works diverge from the ethos embodied in *toppunt* and *stilleven*.

Rembrandt understood that death resides in life from birth, that it grows and matures with it and takes its nourishment from it. Perhaps it was from this awareness that his predilection for what is marked by the harsh impact of time and the world arose:

> From the beginning, he was powerfully drawn to ruin; the poetry of imperfection. He enjoyed tracing the marks left by the bite of worldly experience: the pits and pocks, the red-rimmed eyes and scabby skin which gave the human countenance a mottled richness.[38]

According to Simmel's interpretation, Rembrandt intuitively applied to what he painted the model of the *individuelles Gesetz*, "individual law." Reversing an established philosophical tradition, Simmel claimed that form is not connected to the universal but rather to the individual: "Equipped with this metaphysical uniqueness, form impresses on its bit of matter an individual shape . . . and gives it a meaning of its own."[39]

It is worth noting that from the privilege of individual form there arose that typically Simmelian method—often maliciously defined as "impressionistic"—that is the product of a generic and evanescent "philosophy of life" but is totally coherent with rigorous theoretical issues. This style of thinking has its own "outrageous" strength precisely where it seems the weakest: in the analysis of elements that are resistant to any generalization, irreducible as much to the pure interiority of individual psychology as to the exteriority of social relations.

It does not seem, however, that Simmel was aware of the fact—already discussed by the medieval scholastics and further reinforced by Hegel—that what is individual is ineffable: as soon as it is spoken or thought of, every single "here" and every single "now" loses its specificity and becomes universally valid for every "here" and every "now."[40] The individual law of Simmel seems guaranteed by the notion, in truth not very well explained, that general concepts provide a framework in which to insert individuality.

In his self-portraits, however, Rembrandt's adherence to the law of individuality appears full and free of residue, because individuality carries with it the contingency of life:

> Rembrandt has been accused of "lacking form" because one perfectly naturally equates form with general form. . . . The form, as worked through by Rembrandt, corresponds exactly and exclusively to the life of the respective individual. It lives

and dies with him—in a solidarity that does not permit a general validity or tolerate a different specialization beyond that individual.[41]

"Res Singulares"

At the level of perception via the senses, the preservation of persons and things takes place through art, but at the conceptual level it takes place through philosophy. For Spinoza it was the gaze of the mind—which he considered *sub specie aeternitatis*—that changes and reorients their meaning; it transforms them into things to love and "bless" thanks to their singularity, to their being specific nodes of cognitive and affective relationships. Everything is stripped of its isolation and connected to God (to all of nature) through *amor intellectualis*, which embraces, loves, and preserves individual things, *res singulares*, in their own being.

Although he was reproducing the ideas of a marginal heretical sect from the time of the Reformation, the Swiss writer Gottfried Keller showed in *Ursula*, one of his Zurich Novellas, how everything is connected in an analogous way to the life of the Whole—in this case to the Christian God, pantheistically interpreted:

> He is in the dust of this floor and in the salt of the sea. He melts from the roof with the snow, we hear him dripping, and he gleams as filth in the street. He switches his tail with the fish in the depths of the water, and looks afar with the eye of the hawk that flies high in the air.[42]

Taking an apple and holding it up before him, the peasant "prophet" of the novella says:

> "Hallo, you funny little Lord God; you've fled hither, are sitting in this apple and thinking I won't find you? . . . Look,

brethren and sisters, how the apple begins to shine with inward light, see how it swells on my hands and becomes a world?"[43]

From another point of view, things also speak to those who know how to question them poetically, as in the case of stones and herbs in the only story written by the poet Paul Celan, "*Gespräch im Gebirge*" ("Conversation in the Mountains"[44]). Nevertheless, for Spinoza it was the thing itself that spoke, according to a strict concatenation of ideas, *more geometrico*. The *res singulares*, on the other hand, must be understood in the context of the totality of nature, which also includes us: "singular things cannot be conceived without God"[45] and "the more we understand particular things, the more we understand God."[46]

To express this last proposition in a plainer way, the more we know and love every individual thing, the more we know and love the world. Once it has reached the highest level of *amor Dei intellectualis*, where intelligence coalesces with feelings (*affectus*), the mind can conceive things *sub specie aeternitatis*; it can see in each thing a node of infinite relationships with the whole of nature. Almost as a collateral benefit, whoever contemplates things in this light feels an increase in joy, an expansion of his own being, because he becomes aware of the fact that things are not dead and that we are part of the nature of which they (and we) are an integral part. Man is not an autonomous "empire within an empire,"[47] and everyone, based on his own "power of existing" (*vis existendi*), participates, to some extent, in the vicissitudes of all of reality.

In the case of still-life painting in particular and of works of art in general, it is as if things were telling us (to paraphrase Horace's *Carpe diem!*): *Carpe aeternitatem in momento!*—Seize life at its best, enjoy things at the right time, feel the fullness of your existence in the world before it declines and slips away. The *memento mori* is not forgotten here, but, as Thomas Merton would say, there are two opposite ways to confront caducity: life slips away between our fingers, but it can slip like sand or like seeds. As a seed it is, indeed, harvested in art, in philosophy, and in any other successful transformation of objects into things.

Faced with the revelation of *aeternitas*, the life of things triumphs, along with our own and that of other men. Everything that involves us through the affective knowledge of the *res singulares* releases us from the extortion of those institutions that turn caducity and the fear of death into a political and religious instrument of control. In this sense, "A free man thinks of nothing less than of death, and his wisdom is a meditation, not on death, but on life." ("*Homo liber de nulla re minus, quam de morte cogitat, et ejus sapientia non mortis, sed vitae meditatio est.*")[48]

We are struck by this feeling of *plenitudo vitae* when the opaque veil of daily experience is torn away, suddenly and momentarily. At that moment, "*sentimus, experimurque, nos aeternos esse*" ("we sense and experience that we are eternal"); we feel in ourselves and in the world, without being able to prove it, the presence of a fullness outside time: "nor can eternity be defined by time, or have any relation to time. Nevertheless, we feel and know that we are eternal."[49] Perhaps for us such fullness exists only in the logic of desire, but that does not mean that it cannot serve as a yardstick to judge the inadequacy and the banality of what, though proffered, does not satisfy us.

In the age of the "sex appeal of the inorganic," of mass production and the greatest waste of intelligence and life, is it still meaningful to appeal to the philosophy of Spinoza and to make an effort to look at things *sub specie aeternitatis*? And can the Dutch *stilleven*, with its pathos for *toppunt*, set an example for us, who live among objects that seem to have lost their ability to last and have taken on the appearance of evanescent simulacra?

Making Things Speak

The answer to these and other questions depends on our willingness to reorient ourselves within the horizon of contemporaneity, reworking an art of existence analogous to the *techne tou biou* ("craft of life") of the ancients but capable of including the life of things. The Classic *diakosmesis* (the process of introducing order and giving sense and beauty to the world, thereby giving sense and beauty to ourselves) thus receives supplementary energy capable of breaking the perverse connection between the "sex appeal of the inorganic" and its correlate, man as a "sentient thing."

Reinterpreted outside their original context—thanks to the surplus of meaning that characterizes both great philosophy and great art—the teachings of Spinoza and the example of *stilleven* become effective antidotes to the rapid, fleeting consumption of goods without "love," and they serve as theoretical bridges and ideal models to restore the transit, for long impervious or interrupted, between people and objects.

Independently of Spinoza or *stilleven*, through things we become aware of the fact that not everything is solved within the confines of our inner selves, in a subjective freedom without the constraints of dependency. In their refusal to be devoured and absorbed by the subject, things force us to give up the mistaken belief that individual identity is a monad or a self-awareness that bites its own tail. Things urge us to listen to reality, to let it in through the window of the psyche, so as to ventilate an otherwise asphyxiated interiority—which, nonetheless, without knowing it, contains both others and the "external world," albeit in the crude form of shadowy presences or banal stereotypes. Paradoxically, things tell more about us—about what makes us ourselves—the more we let them express themselves in their own language: the language of the *pragma*, the *res*, or *Sache*, and, at times, with a more authoritative voice, the language of the *auto to pragma* and *Sache selbst*.

Gradually releasing their own meaning without exhausting it, living their own life in their own way, things share a bond of antagonistic complicity with us: they are useful; they remain close and indispensable, but, challenging our greedy or lazy tendency to usurp them without leaving any trace, they retain their own substance. Only this relative elusiveness can bring us back to ourselves and allow us to breathe the aura, described by Benjamin, that connects proximity and distance, familiarity and strangeness: "Everything that has been made in this way, out of love and necessity, leads a life of its own, leads into a strange new territory and returns with us."[50]

Things lead us, agonistically, to rise above the inconsistency and mediocrity into which we would fall if we did not invest in them—tacitly reciprocated—thoughts, fantasies, and emotions. They are things because we think about them; because we know them and we love them in their singularity; because, in contrast to objects, we do not claim that we use them only as instruments or to cancel out their otherness; and because, as happens in art, we remove them from their precarious condition in space and time, transforming them into "miniatures of eternity" that contain the complete fullness of existence.

Our relationship with things resembles, to a lesser degree, the love between people: to love someone, the other must be another me, equal to me, so that I can be in tune with him, but, at the same time, he must be different from me, so that we complement each other. If the other were too similar to me, a kind of perfect copy, I would not need him; if he were too different, he would leave my orbit and would become unreachable. Shifting and swinging its mobile center of gravity, love accomplishes the miracle of enhancing freedom in the bond and the bond in freedom, of denying the possession of the other and maintaining, while its perfection lasts, a reciprocal autonomy between those who love.

To rescue objects from their insignificance or from their purely instrumental use means to understand better ourselves and the events in which we are engaged—since things establish synapses of meaning both between the different segments of the individual and collective story and between human civilizations and nature. Things live if we are able to develop and to render almost spontaneous a sort of semiotic system similar to the one used by physicians to interpret symptoms: to recognize in what is most important to us its history in relation to man and its origin in relation to nature.

Considered with sympathetic attention, any thing can yield different paths of curiosity (and here I am using the word "curiosity" in its noble, etymological sense: from the Latin *cura*, denoting zeal or desire to learn) and research: a rag doll or porcelain doll may lead us, with imagination and inquiry, to place it in a period preceding the invention of plastic, to situate it in the history of toys, to think about the differences in the ways that females and males are raised, or perhaps to recall episodes of family history. An old military uniform found in a junk shop can reveal—by the type of cloth, insignia, or ranks—the membership of the wearer to a particular armed force and period, and it can be mentally placed in the history of a nation or in the history of fashion. As noted by Max Weber, the buttons on the uniform worn by the king of Prussia during the Battle of Sadowa (also known as the

Battle of Königgrätz) seem irrelevant, but if the point of view of military history is replaced by that of the history of fashion, those buttons will be more important than the outcome of the battle.

If we overcome the tendency to remain centered on ourselves, without "reaching out" toward what might renew us, then the stories of things, with their cargo of symbols and stratifications, might appear so vast and rich that we could easily get lost. We must, therefore, take into account a warning similar to the one expressed by Nietzsche in the second part of *Thoughts Out of Season*: an excess of historical memory is likely to flatten out the past and paralyze our momentum toward the future; thus the desire to embrace and understand too many things, senselessly piling them up, is likely to encumber our capacity to love and understand any. Aristotle was right: "The man who has many friends has no friend."[51]

To sum up, things live under certain conditions: if we let them exist alongside us, and together with us, without attempting to absorb them; if we juxtapose our lives to those of others; if, through things, we open ourselves to the world and let it flow into us; if we pour ourselves into the world to make it more meaningful and in harmony with ideals of general interest that we can discuss together—also thanks to our own *diakosmesis*; if we cultivate an attitude that can overcome the opposition between an interiority that is closed and self-referential and an exteriority that is inert and secondhand; if, conscious of the fact that we cannot take anything with us to the afterlife—because, as a German proverb says, "the last dress has no pockets"—we stop giving priority to relationships of exclusive possession, to accumulating and controlling objects; if, looking at the original meaning of eternity as the fullness of life, we give up living just for the moment; if we move away from the exhibitionism of the logo and the culture of waste to a simple, essential relationship with things; if we succeed in recognizing in each thing the nature of the *res singularis*, invested as such with intelligence, symbols, and emotions; if we continuously broaden our mental and emotional horizons, we can avoid losing the awareness of the unfathomable depths of the world, of others, and of ourselves. What Heraclitus argued about the *psyche* ("One would never discover the limits of the soul, should one traverse every road—so deep a measure does it possess")[52] also applies to the things of the world, in their historical and personal significance, and in the as yet only partially explored complexity of the matter of the universe—of which our body and objects in the universe are composed and to which our subjectivity is inextricably joined.

The brevity of life and the causality of birth, which enclose everyone in a limited time and space, allow us to come into contact with only a limited number of things. The decision to know and to care for some things, without precluding the understanding of other things, implies not only an attitude of constant attention to the world and to people, a willingness to learn, and a desire to love; it also implies an ethos and even a political stance: that of contributing to making a *respublica* out of the society that fate has thrust upon us.

NOTES

1. OBJECTS AND THINGS

1. Virgil, *Eclogues, Georgics, Aeneid*, trans. H. Rushton Fair-clough, rev. G. P. Goold, Loeb Classical Library 64 (Cambridge, Mass.: Harvard University Press, 1999–2000), 519–525.

2. Marcel Proust, *Remembrance of Things Past*, vol. 3, *The Guermantes Way*, trans. C. K. Scott Moncrieff, ed. Paul Bowden (2012).

3. Virgil, *Aeneid*, trans. Theodore C. Williams (Boston: Houghton Mifflin, 1910), IV, lines 522–528.

4. Ovid, *Metamorphoses*, trans. Brookes More (Boston: Cornhill, 1922), VII, lines 185–187.

5. Hermann Broch, *The Death of Virgil*, trans. Jean Starr Untermeyer (New York: Vintage, 1995).

6. Marcel Proust, *Remembrance of Things Past*, vol. 1, *Swann's Way*.

7. Ibid.

8. Jean-Paul Sartre, *The Imaginary*, ed. Arlette Elkaïm-Sartre and Jonathan Webber, trans. Jonathan Webber (London: Routledge, 2004), 9.

9. See Maurice Merleau-Ponty, "Eye and Mind," in *The Primacy of Perception and Other Essays on Phenomenological Psychology, the Philosophy of Art, History, and Politics*, trans. Carleton Dallery (Evanston, Ill.: Northwestern University Press, 1964), 154ff.

10. See Harvey Molotch, *Where Stuff Comes From: How Toasters, Toilets, Cars, Computers, and Many Other Things Come to Be as They Are* (New York: Routledge, 2003), 7.

11. See Raymond Geuss, *Public Goods, Private Goods* (Princeton, N.J.: Princeton University Press, 2001), 34ff.

12. See Aristotle *Topics* I, 18, 108a, 20–25; and, more generally, Gilbert Romeyer-Dherbey, *Les choses mêmes: la pensée du réel chez Aristote* (Lausanne: L'Age d'Homme, 1983).

13. Aristotle, *Metaphysics* 984 b 9, 984 a 18.

14. See, among others, Alfredo Ferrarin, *Hegel and Aristotle* (Cambridge: Cambridge University Press, 2001), 47–54.

15. See Edmund Husserl, *Logical Investigations*, trans. J. N. Findlay, ed. Dermot Moran (London: Routledge, 2001); see also Stefano Catucci, "Le cose stesse: appunti su un'autocritica trascendentale della fenomenologia," *Leitmotiv* 3 (2003): 43–44, http://www.ledonline.it /leitmotiv/Allegati/leitmotivo30303.pdf.

16. See also Hans Blumenberg, *Zu den Sachen und zurück* (Frankfurt: Suhrkamp, 2002).

17. Dante, *Paradise*, trans. Robert Hollander (New York: Doubleday, 2007), IV, 124–129; see also G. W. F. Hegel, *The Encyclopaedia of Logic: Part 1 of the Encyclopaedia of Philosophical Sciences with the Zusätze*, ed. Theodore F. Geraets, W. A. Suchting, and H. S. Harris (Indianapolis: Hackett, 1991), §440 Z.

18. G. W. F. Hegel, *The Phenomenology of Spirit (The Phenomenology of Mind)*, trans. J. B. Baillie (Lawrence, Kan.: Digireads.com, 2009), 1:33.

19. Ibid., 1:17.

20. *Hesiod's Works and Days: A Translation and Commentary for the Social Sciences*, trans. David W. Tandy and Walter C. Neale (Berkeley: University of California Press, 1996), line 405.

21. See Hegel, *Phenomenology of Spirit*, 1:177–195; and, from different perspectives, Ernst Bloch, "Subjekt-Objekt. Eläuterungen zu Hegel," in *Gesamtausgabe*, vol. 8 (Berlin: Aufbau Verlag, 1951); Johannes Agnoli, *Subversive Theorie: "die Sache selbst" und ihre Geschichte: eine Berliner Vorlesung*, ed. Christoph Hühne (Freiburg: Ça ira Verlag, 1996); and, above all, Étienne Balibar, "Zur 'Sache Selbst':

Comune e universale nella 'Fenomenologia' di Hegel," *Iride* 52, no. 20 (December 2007): 553–558.

22. G. W. F. Hegel, *The Science of Logic*, trans. George Di Giovanni (Cambridge: Cambridge University Press, 2010), 25, 17.

23. Hegel, *Encyclopedia of Philosophical Knowledge*, §246 Z.

24. Aristotle, *Metaphysics* VII, 3, 1028 b 36.

25. See Thomas Aquinas, *Summa Theologica* I, q. 29, a. 2.

26. John Locke, *Essay Concerning Human Understanding* (Oxford: Oxford University Press, 1975), II, 23, 1–2.

27. Theodor Adorno, *Minima Moralia: Reflections on a Damaged Life*, trans. E. F. N. Jephcott (London: Verso, 2005), 69.

28. Jean Baudrillard, *The System of Objects*, trans. James Benedict (London: Verso, 2005), 1.

29. Lydia Flem, *The Final Reminder: How I Emptied My Parents' House*, trans. Elfreda Powell (London: Souvenir, 2007), 36.

30. Sigmund Freud, "Mourning and Melancholia," in *The Standard Edition of the Complete Psychological Works of Sigmund Freud*, trans. James Strachey (London: Hogarth Press and the Institute of Psycho-Analysis, 1953–1974), 17:243–258.

31. Fernando Pessoa, *The Book of Disquiet*, trans. Margaret Jull Costa (London: Serpent's Tail, 2010), 143 [219].

32. Benedetto Croce, "Frammenti di etica IV: i trapassati," *Etica e politica* (Rome/Bari: Laterza, 1973), 23–24.

33. Flem, *The Final Reminder*, 29.

34. Ibid., 95–96.

35. See Charles de Brosses, *Du culte des dieux fétiches, ou Parallèle de l'ancienne religion de l'Egypte avec la religion actuelle de la Nigritie* [1760] (Paris: Fayard, 1988); Alfonso Maurizio Iacono, *Teorie del feticismo* (Milan: Giuffré, 1985); Marc Augé, *Le dieu objet* (Paris: Flammarion, 1988).

36. Augé, *Le dieu objet*, 28, 29, 132.

37. Claude Lévi-Strauss, *Introduction to the Work of Marcel Mauss*, trans. Felicity Baker (London: Routledge, 1987), 62–63.

38. Guido Cavalcanti, *The Complete Poems*, trans. Marc Cirigliano (New York: Italica, 1992), 40; see also Francesca Rigotti, *La filosofia delle piccole cose* (Novara: Interlinea, 2004), 45.

39. Franz Kafka, "The Cares of a Family Man," in *Complete Stories*, trans. Willa Muir and Edwin Muir (New York: Schocken, 1971), 269–270; Walter Benjamin, "Franz Kafka: On the Anniversary of His Death," in *Illuminations*, ed. Hannah Arendt, trans. Harry Zohn (New York: Schocken, 2007), 132–134.

40. Kafka, "The Cares of a Family Man," 269–270.

41. Francesco Orlando, *Gli oggetti desueti nelle immagini della letteratura* (Turin: Einaudi, 1997), 3, 6; Umberto Eco, *The Mysterious Flame of Queen Loana*, trans. Geoffrey Brock (San Diego, Calif.: Houghton Mifflin Harcourt, 2005).

42. Jorge Luis Borges, "Things," trans. Stephen Kessler, *New Yorker* (March 22, 1999): 66.

43. Pablo Neruda, "Things," in *Fifty Odes*, trans. George D. Schade (Austin, Tex.: Host, 2001), 27.

44. Ludwig Wittgenstein, "Remarks on Frazer's Golden Bough," *Philosophical Occasions 1912–1951*, ed. James Carl Klagge and Alfred Nordmann (Indianapolis: Hackett, 1993), 131.

45. Wittgenstein, *Philosophical Investigations*, rev. 4th ed., trans. G. E. M. Anscombe, P. M. S. Hacker, and Joachim Schulte (Oxford: Blackwell, 2009), §129.

46. See Norwood Hanson, *Patterns of Discovery: An Inquiry Into the Conceptual Foundations of Science* (Cambridge: Cambridge University Press, 1958), 4–5.

47. Edmund Husserl, *The Crisis of European Sciences and Transcendental Philosophy*, trans. David Carr (Evanston, Ill.: Northwestern University Press, 1970), §§9–10, 55.

48. Merleau-Ponty, "Eye and Mind," 160.

49. In Greek mythology, Procrustes was a smith who stretched people or cut off their legs to get them to fit onto an iron bed; "Procrustean" indicates something that is forced to conform to an arbitrary standard.

50. Edmund Husserl, *Cartesian Meditations: An Introduction to Phenomenology*, trans. Dorion Cairns (The Hague: Martinus Nijhoff, 1977), 18–22.

51. Theodor W. Adorno, *Against Epistemology: A Metacritique*, trans. Willis Domingo (Cambridge: Polity, 2013), 196.

52. Gaston Bachelard, *The Formation of the Scientific Mind*, trans. M. McAllester Jones (Bolton: Clinamen, 2002), 70. See also *The New Scientific Spirit*, trans. A. Goldhammer (Boston: Beacon, 1984).

53. Merleau-Ponty, "Eye and Mind," 188.

54. Edmund Husserl, "Phenomenology as Transcendental Philosophy: 5. The Basic Approach of Phenomenology," in *The Essential Husserl: Basic Writings in Transcendental Phenomenology*, ed. Donn Welton (Bloomington: Indiana University Press, 1999), 84 (§55).

55. Husserl, *The Crisis of European Sciences*, 157–158.

56. Edmund Husserl, *Logical Investigations*, vol. 2, investigation VI, "Elements of a Phenomenological Elucidation of Knowledge."

57. Giacomo Leopardi, *Zibaldone*, ed. Michael Caesar and Franco D'Intino, trans. Kathleen Baldwin (New York: Farrar, Straus, and Giroux, 2013), 132.

58. Edmund Husserl, *The Basic Problems of Phenomenology*, trans. Ingo Farin and James G. Hart (Dordrecht: Springer, 2006), 6, 7.

59. Edmund Husserl, *Ideas Pertaining to a Pure Phenomenology*, trans. F. Kersten (The Hague: Nartinus Mijhoff, 1982), 52, 53.

60. Hanson, *Patterns of Discovery*, 25.

61. Husserl, *Ideas Pertaining to a Pure Phenomenology,* 53.

62. Georg Simmel, *Georg Simmel, 1858–1918: A Collection of Essays*, ed. Kurt H. Wolff, trans. Rudolph H. Weingartner (Columbus: Ohio State University Press, 1959), 268–269, 273, 274.

63. See Patrizia Cipolletta, *La tecnica e le cose: assonanze e dissonanze tra Bloch e Heidegger* (Milan: Franco Angeli Editore, 2001), 99–100; and, more generally, Manfred Riedel, "Krug, Glas und frühe Begegnung. Zum Auftakt von Blochs Philosophie," in *Ich bin. Aber ich habe mich nich. Darum werden wir erst: Perspektiven der Philosophie Ernst Blochs*, ed. Jan Robert Bloch (Frankfurt am Main: Suhrkamp, 1997).

64. See Ernst Bloch, *The Spirit of Utopia*, trans. Anthony A. Nassar (Stanford, Calif.: Stanford University Press, 2000), 7–8.

65. Martin Heidegger, "The Thing," in *Poetry, Language, Thought*, ed. and trans. Albert Hofstadter (New York: HarperCollins, 2001), 172–173.

66. Cipolletta, *La tecnica e le cose*, 125; see also 134–143.

67. Aristotle, *Metaphysics* I, 2, 982 b 13–14.

68. Martin Heidegger, *Being and Time*, trans. Joan Stambaugh and Dennis J. Schmidt (Albany, N.Y.: State University of New York Press, 1996), 66.

69. Martin Heidegger, *Zollikon Seminars*, ed. by M. Bos, trans. R. Askay and F. Mayr (Evanston, Ill.: Northwestern University Press, 2001). See also Vincenzo Costa, "Essere nel mondo," in *Storia dell'ontologia*, ed. Maurizio Ferraris (Milan: Bompiani, 2008), 266–267.

70. Martin Heidegger, "The Fieldpath," trans. Berrit Mexia, *Journal of Chinese Philosophy* 13 (1986): 455–458.

71. See Martin Heidegger, "The Origin of the Work of Art," in *The Art of Art History: A Critical Anthology*, new ed., ed. Donald Preziosi (Oxford: Oxford University Press, 2009), 284–295; and Heidegger, "The Thing."

72. See Jean-Luc Nancy, *À l'ecoute* (Paris: Galilée, 2004), 22.

73. Walter Benjamin, *The Work of Art in the Age of Its Technological Reproducibility and Other Writings on Media*, trans. Edmund Jephcott and Harry Zohn (Cambridge, Mass.: The Belknap Press of Harvard University Press, 2008), 23. See also Marleen Stössel, *Aura, das vergessene Menschliche: zu Sprache und Erfahrung bei Walter Benjamin* (Munich: Hanser, 1983); and Birgit Recki, *Aura und Autonomie: zur Subjektivität der Kunst bei Walter Benjamin and Theodor W. Adorno* (Würzburg: Königshausen & Neumann, 1988).

74. Heidegger, "The Thing," 161ff.

75. Benjamin, *The Work of Art in the Age of Its Technological Reproducibility*, 22.

2. OPENING UP TO THE WORLD

1. Andrea Borsari et al., *L'esperienza delle cose* (Genoa: Marietti, 1992), 7.

2. Daniel Roche, *A History of Everyday Things: The Birth of Consumption in France, 1600–1800*, trans. Brian Pearce (Cambridge: Cambridge University Press, 2008), 181.

3. Immanuel Kant, *The Critique of Pure Reason*, trans. J. M. D. Meiklejohn (Hazelton: Pennsylvania State University, 2010), 171.

4. See John Locke, *An Essay Concerning Human Understanding* (London: William Tegg & Company, 1853), 230–231.

5. Giambattista Vico, *The New Science of Giambattista Vico*, trans. Thomas Goddard Bergin and Max Harold Fisch (Ithaca, NY: Cornell University Press, 1984), 93.

6. Maurizio Ferraris, ed., *Storia dell'ontologia* (Milan: Bompiani, 2008), 480; John R. Searle, *The Construction of Social Reality* (New York: Free Press, 1995). See also Maurizio Ferraris, *Ontologia* (Naples: Guida, 2003); and Maurizio Ferraris, *Dove sei? Ontologia del telefonino* (Milan: Bompiani, 2005). Ferraris's "A Cocktail of Searle" (2006), is available at http://www.labont.com/public/Archivio%20Ferraris/ DocHome/A_Cocktail_of_Searle.pdf.

7. See Achille C. Varzi, *Parole, oggetti, eventi e altri argomenti di metafisica* (Rome: Carocci, 2001), 91–120; and Achille C. Varzi, "La natura e l'identità dei materiali," *Manuale di filosofia analitica*, ed. A. Coliva (Rome: Carocci, 2007).

8. See Richard Sennett, *The Craftsman* (New Haven, Conn.: Yale University Press, 2008), 119ff.; and Suzanne Staubach, *Clay: The History and Evolution of Humankind's Relationship with Earth's Most Primal Element* (Berkeley: University of California Press, 2005).

9. Wilhelm Dilthey, *Selected Works*, ed. Rudolf A. Makkreel and Frithjof Rodi (Princeton, N.J.: Princeton University Press, 2002), 3:229.

10. Max Scheler, *The Human Place in the* Cosmos, trans. Manfred S. Frings (Evanston, Ill.: Northwestern University Press, 2009), 33.

11. See Jorge Luis Borges, "The Maker," in *Collected Fictions*, trans. Andrew Hurley (New York: Penguin, 1998), 314.

12. Vladimir Jankélévitch, *L'irreversibilité et la nostalgie* (Paris: Flammarion, 1974), 399ff.

13. See Fernand Braudel, *Civilization and Capitalism, 15th–18th Centuries*, 3 vols., trans. Siân Reynolds (New York: Harper & Row, 1982–1984), among the founders of this trend.

14. See Roberto Esposito, *Third Person: Politics of Life and Philosophy of the Impersonal*, trans. Zakiya Hanafi (Cambridge: Polity, 2012).

15. Daniele Del Giudice, "Gli oggetti, la letteratura, la memoria," in Borsari et al., *L'esperienza delle cose*, 95; see also Jean Baudrillard, *The System of Objects*, trans. James Benedict (London: Verso, 2005), 14.

16. Augustine of Hippo, *Soliloquies: Immortality of the Soul*, trans. Gerald Watson (Warminster: Aris & Phillips, 1990), I, 1, 4.

17. Lucretius, *On the Nature of Things*, trans. Robert Allison (London: A. L. Humphreys, 1919), I, 311–321.

18. Ezio Manzini, "Il mondo che sembra: l'identità incerta del nuovo mondo artificiale," in Borsari et al., *L'esperienza delle cose*, 81.

19. See Jean Baudrillard, *The Consumer Society: Myths and Structures*, trans. Chris Turner (London: Sage, 1998), 47.

20. Bachisio Bandinu and Gaspare Barbiellini Amidei, *Il re è un feticcio: romanzo di cose* (Nuoro: Ilisso, 2003), 31.

21. Ibid., 31.

22. See Aldona Jonaitis, ed., *Chiefly Feasts: The Enduring Kwakiutl Potlatch* (Seattle: University of Washington Press; New York: American Museum of Natural History, 1991), 229, 247, photo 5.19.

23. Elias Canetti, *Crowds and Power*, trans. Carol Stewart (New York: Farrar, Straus and Giroux, 1984), 19.

24. This view is sustained by Louis Dumont, *From Mandeville to Marx: The Genesis and Triumph of Economic Ideology* (Chicago: University of Chicago Press, 1977), 81; and by Alfonso Maurizio Iacono, *Teorie del feticismo* (Milan: Giuffré, 1985), 15.

25. The eponymous protagonist of the novel published in 1889 by Giuseppe Verga; Gesualdo rises from the status of a peasant to that of a wealthy landowner.

26. See Hrant Pasdermadjian, *The Department Store: Its Origins, Evolution, and Economics* (London: Newman, 1954), 125; Michael B. Miller, *The Bon Marché: Bourgeois Culture and the Department Store, 1869–1920* (Princeton, N.J.: Princeton University Press, 1994); Rosalind H. Williams, *Dream World: Mass Consumption in Late Nineteenth-Century France* (Berkeley: University of California Press, 1982); Remo Bodei, *Geometria delle passioni* (Milan: Feltrinelli, 1991), 13–17; Marco Belpoliti, *Il tramezzino del dinosauro: 100 oggetti, comportamenti e manie della vita quotidiana* (Parma: Guanda, 2008), 181–182.

27. Baudrillard, *Consumer Society*, 25; see also Baudrillard, "The System of Objects," 1.

28. Baudrillard, *Consumer Society*, 192.

29. See Remo Bodei, *Paesaggi sublimi: Gli uomini davanti alla natura selvaggia* (Milan: Bompiani, 2008), 145–182.

30. Belpoliti, *Il tramezzino del dinosauro*, 9, 10.

31. John Maynard Keynes, *A Treatise on Probability* (London: Routledge, 1963), 42.

32. Roche, *A History of Everyday Things*, 2.

33. Baudrillard, *The Consumer Society*, 1998, 196; see also Baudrillard, "The System of Objects."

34. Francesca Rigotti, *Il pensiero delle cose* (Milan: Apogeo, 2007), 22.

35. See Roland Barthes, *Mythologies*, trans. Annette Lavers (London: Paladin, 1972); Baudrillard, "The System of Objects," 69ff.; and Jerôme Garcin, ed., *Nouvelles Mythologies* (Paris: Seuil, 2007).

36. See Myron W. Krueger, *Artificial Reality II* (Reading, Mass.: Addison-Wesley, 1991).

37. Mary Douglas and Baron C. Isherwood, *The World of Goods: Toward an Anthropology of Consumption* (London: Routledge, 1996), 43.

38. See François Dagognet, *Éloge de l'object: pour une philosophie de la merchandise* (Paris: Librairie Philosophique J. Vrin, 1989); Roberta Sassatelli, *Consumer Culture: History, Theory, and Politics* (Los Angeles: Sage, 2007).

39. George Perec, *Things: A Story of the Sixties*, trans. David Bellos (Boston: Godine, 1990).

40. Maurizio Vitta, *Il disegno delle cose: storia degli oggetti e teoria del design* (Naples: Liguori, 1996), 337.

41. See Georg Simmel, "The Philosophy of Fashion," in *Simmel on Culture*, ed. David Frisby and Mike Featherstone (London: Sage, 1997), 187–206.

42. See Elena Esposito, *I paradossi della moda: originalità e transitorietà nella società moderna* (Bologna: Baskerville, 2004).

43. Act 2, Scene 2; see also Elena Esposito, *I paradossi della moda*.

44. Rainer Maria Rilke, *Letters of Rainer Maria Rilke, 1910–1026*, trans. Jane Bannard Greene and M. D. Herter Norton (New York: Norton, 1948), 2:374–375.

45. Roche, *A History of Everyday Things*, 255.

46. Antonio Serra, *A Short Treatise on the Wealth and Poverty of Nations* (1613), ed. Sophus A. Reinert, trans. Jonathan Hunt (London: Anthem, 2011).

47. A Socratic dialogue about household management and agriculture and one of the earliest literary works about economics in its original meaning of household management.

48. Otto Brummer, "Das ganze Haus und die alteuropäische Ökonomie," *Neue Wege der Verfassungs-und Sozialgeschichte*, ed. O. Brummer (Göttingen: Vandenhoeck, 1968), 103–127; Gabriella Bodei Giglioni, "L'oikos: realtà familiare e realtà economica," in *I Greci: storia, cultura, arte*, ed. Salvatore Settis (Turin: Einaudi, 1996), II, 1, 735–754.

49. Roche, *A History of Everyday Things*, 83–84.

50. Renata Ago, *Il gusto delle cose: una storia degli oggetti nella Roma del Seicento* (Rome: Donzelli, 2006), xvii–xxii, 123–126.

51. Gaston Bachelard, *The Poetics of Space: The Classic Look at How We Experience Intimate Places*, trans. Maria Jolas (Boston: Beacon, 1994), 7; Antonella Tarpino, *Geografie della memoria: case, rovine, oggetti quotidiani* (Turin: Einaudi, 2008), 40, 47ff.

52. Baudrillard, *The System of Objects*, 15–17.

53. See Sennett, *The Craftsman*, 244–267; and Toby Faber, *Stradivarius: Five Violins, One Cello, and a Genius* (London: Macmillan, 2004).

54. Remo Bodei, *Le forme del bello* (Bologna: Il Mulino, 1995), 74.

55. Walter Benjamin, *The Arcades Project*, ed. Rolf Teidemann (Cambridge, Mass.: The Belknap Press of Harvard University Press, 1999), 79, 63.

56. Mario Perniola, *The Sex Appeal of the Inorganic: Philosophies of Desire in the Modern World*, trans. Massimo Verdicchio (New York: Continuum, 2004), 48.

57. Ernesto L. Francalanci, *Estetica degli oggetti* (Bologna: Il Mulino, 2006), 9; see also 63–64.

58. See Harvey Molotch, *Where Stuff Comes From: How Toasters, Toilets, Cars, Computers, and Many Other Things Come to Be as They Are* (New York: Routledge, 2003), 42–74, for the example of automobiles.

59. See Naomi Klein, *No Space, No Choice, No Jobs, No Logo: Taking Aim at the Brand Bullies* (New York: Picador, 2002); Vanni Codeluppi, *Il potere della marca: Disney, McDonald's, Nike e le altre* (Turin: Bollati Boringhieri, 2001); Scott Lash and Celia Lury, *Global Culture Industry: The Mediation of Things* (Cambridge: Polity, 2007).

60. See Sennet, *The Craftsman*, 100, 273.

61. See Fulvio Carmagnola, *Luoghi della qualità: estetica e tecnologia nel postindustriale* (Milan: Domus Academy, 1991); Fulvio Carmagnola and Mauro Ferraresi, *Merci di culto: ipermerce e società mediale* (Rome: Castelvecchi, 1999); Sennett, *The Craftsman*.

62. See Molotch, *Where Stuff Comes From*, 2.

63. See, among the most well-known studies, Donna Jeanne Haraway, *Simians, Cyborgs, and Women: The Reinvention of Nature* (New York: Routledge, 1991); Katherine Hayles, *How We Became Posthuman: Virtual Bodies in Cybernetics, Literature, and Informatics* (Chicago: University of Chicago Press, 1999); and Roberto Marchesini, *Post-human: verso nuovi modelli di esistenza* (Turin: Bollati Boringhieri, 2002).

64. Giovanni Anceschi, ed., *Il progetto delle interfacce: oggetti colloquiali e protesi virtuali* (Milan: Domus Academy, 2002), 221; cited by Francalanci in *Estetica degli oggetti*, 22.

65. See Michael Polanyi, *The Tacit Dimension* (Garden City, N.Y.: Doubleday, 1967), 9–11.

66. See François Jullien, *Un sage est sans idée ou l'autre de la philosophie* (Paris: Seuil, 1998).

67. Gabriella Pasqualotto, *Taccuino giapponese* (Udine: Forum, 2008), 75.

68. See Martin Heidegger, "The Fieldpath," trans. Berrit Mexia, *Journal of Chinese Philosophy* 13 (1986): 455–458.

69. Maurice Merleau-Ponty, *Nature: Course Notes from the Collège de France*, ed. Dominique Séglard; trans. Robert Vallier (Evanston, Ill.: Northwestern University Press, 2003), 125–126.

70. René Descartes, *Meditations on First Philosophy, with Selections from the Objections and Replies*, ed. and trans. John Cottingham (Cambridge: Cambridge University Press, 1996), 20.

71. Ibid., 20.

72. Ibid., 21.

73. See Bodei, *Le forme del bello*, 23–32.

74. Gilbert Simondon, *On the Mode of Existence of Technical Objects*, trans. Niniam Mellamphy (London, Ontario: University of Western Ontario, 1980).

75. Hannah Arendt, *The Life of the Mind*, ed. Mary McCarthy (New York: Harcourt Brace Jovanovich, 1978), 69.

76. Walter Benjamin, *The Work of Art in the Age of Its Technological Reproducibility and Other Writings on Media*, trans. Edmund Jephcott and Harry Zohn (Cambridge, Mass.: The Belknap Press of Harvard University Press, 2008), 24.

77. Taken from Bonnefoy's own introduction to the 1972 French edition of *L'Arrière-pays*. The English translation, by Stephen Romer, was published in 2012 (London: Seagull).

78. Johann Wolfgang von Goethe, "*Zueignung*" (dedication to the drama *Faust*), lines 31–32, in *Selected Poetry*, trans. David Luke (London: Penguin, 2005), 49.

79. Giorgio Caproni, "Return," in *Wall of the Earth: Essential Poets Series*, trans. Pasquale Verdicchio (Toronto: Guernica, 1992), 81.

80. Ernst Bloch, *Traces*, trans. Anthony A. Nassar (Stanford, Calif.: Stanford University Press, 2006), 71.

81. Hans Christian Andersen, *The Steadfast Tin Soldier*, trans. Jean Hersholt (New York: Macmillan, 1927).

82. Directed by John Lasseter, 1995.

83. Giorgio Agamben, *Stanze: Word and Phantasm in Western Culture*, trans. Ronald L. Martinez (Minneapolis: University of Minnesota Press, 1992), 51; Francalanci, *Estetica degli oggetti*, 9.

84. Painted in 1886 and now preserved in the Van Gogh Museum in Amsterdam.

85. Martin Heidegger, "The Origin of the Work of Art," in *Basic Writings*, ed. Farrell Krell and Taylor Carman (New York: HarperCollins, 2008), 159–160.

86. Meyer Schapiro, "The Still Life as a Personal Object: A Note on Heidegger and Van Gogh," in *The Art of Art History: A Critical Anthology*, ed. Donald Preziosi (Oxford: Oxford University Press, 2009), 296–300. On the contrast between Schapiro, the uprooted citizen, and Heidegger, the sedentary countryman who feels the archaic call of the earth, see Jacques Derrida, "Restitutions of the Truth in Pointing [*Pointure*]," in *The Truth in Painting*, trans. Geoffrey Bennington and Ian McLeod (Chicago: University of Chicago Press, 1987), 255–382 (Derrida's essay is also included in Preziosi, *The Art of Art History*); and Andrea Pinotti, *Estetica della pittura* (Bologna: Il Mulino, 2007), 129–134. For other aspects, see Rigotti, *Il pensiero delle cose*, 53–54.

87. Martin Heidegger, "Remarks on Art-Sculpture-Space," quoted in Andrew Mitchell, *Heidegger Among the Sculptors: Body, Space, and the Art of Dwelling* (Stanford, Calif.: Stanford University Press, 2010), 52.

88. Maurice Merleau-Ponty, "Eye and Mind," in *The Primacy of Perception and Other Essays on Phenomenological Psychology, the Philosophy of Art, History, and Politics*, trans. Carleton Dallery (Evanston, Ill.: Northwestern University Press, 1964), 161.

89. Bloch, *Traces*, 136.

90. Maurice Merleau-Ponty, *The Visible and the Invisible*, ed. Claude Lefort, trans. Alphonso Lingis (Evanston, Ill.: Northwestern University Press, 1968), 133.

91. Maurice Merleau-Ponty, "Cézanne's Doubt," in *Merleau-Ponty Aesthetics Reader: Philosophy and Painting*, ed. and trans. Michael B. Smith (Evanston, Ill.: Northwestern University Press, 1993), 59ff.

92. Ibid., 66.

93. Merleau-Ponty, "Eye and Mind," 163.

3. LIVING NATURE

1. Also called "static life" or "silent life" in other languages, but always involving the idea of something living and natural, not inert: *stilleven, Stilleben, natura morta*.

2. See the exhibition catalogue by Alan Chong, Wouter Kloek, and Celeste Brusati, *Still-Life Paintings from the Netherlands 1550–1720* (Amsterdam: Rijksmuseum; Cleveland: Cleveland Museum of Art, 1999).

3. See Norbert Schneider, *Still Life: Still Life Painting in the Early Modern Period*, trans. Hugh Beyer (Cologne: Taschen, 2009), 7.

4. Charles Sterling, *Still Life Painting from Antiquity to the Twentieth Century*, 2nd rev. ed. (New York: Harper & Row, 1981), 27, where "rhopography" is defined as the depiction of insignificant objects; Norman Bryson, *Looking at the Overlooked: Four Essays on Still Life* (Cambridge, Mass.: Harvard University Press, 1990).

5. From Act 1, "*piccole cose umili e silenziose.*"

6. Elisa Acanfora, "Le origini della natura morta," in *La natura morta italiana da Caravaggio al Settecento* (Milan: Electa, 2003).

7. Sterling, *Still Life Painting*, 13.

8. René Girard, *La voix méconnue du réel: une théorie des mythes archaïques et modernes* (Paris: Grasset & Fasquelles, 2002).

9. Plotinus, *Enneads* IV, 4, 37.

10. Pierre Hadot, *What Is Ancient Philosophy?*, trans. Michael Chase (Cambridge, Mass.: Harvard University Press, 2004), 222.

11. Karl Jaspers, *Nietzsche: An Introduction to the Understanding of His Philosophical Activity* (Baltimore, Md.: Johns Hopkins University Press, 1997), 199.

12. Vilém Flusser, *Dinge und Undinge. Phänomenologische Skizzen* (Munich: Hanser, 1993).

13. Arundhati Roy, *The God of Small Things* (New York: Harper-Collins, 1998).

14. Lisa Bortolotti, *La natura morta: storia, artisti, opera* (Florence: Giunti, 2005).

15. Judikje Kiers and Fieke Tissink, *The Golden Age of Dutch Art: Painting, Sculpture, Decorative Art* (London: Thames and Hudson, 2000), 27–34.

16. Simon Shama, *The Embarrassment of Riches: An Interpretation of Dutch Culture in the Golden Age* (Berkeley: University of California Press, 1988); Julie Berger Hochstrasser, *Still Life and Trade in*

the Dutch Golden Age (New Haven, Conn.: Yale University Press, 2007).

17. Hochstrasser, *Still Life and Trade in the Dutch Golden Age.*

18. José Ortega y Gasset, *Meditations on Quixote*, trans. Evelyn Rugg and Diego Marín (Champaign: University of Illinois Press, 2000), 32.

19. Also, though from a very different perspective, see Jean-Luc Nancy, *Le regard du portrait* (Paris: Galileé, 2002), 50. For an analysis of this posthumous portrait in the context of art history, see Lia Bellingeri, *Genovesino* (Galatina, Lecce: Mario Congedo Editore, 2007), 20 and plate 20.

20. Elena Esposito, *I paradossi della moda: originalità e transitorietà nella società moderna* (Bologna: Baskerville, 2004).

21. Jeanne Hersch, *L'être et la forme* (Neuchâtel: Éditions de la Baconnière, 1946); Jeanne Hersch, *Textes* (Fribourg: Le Feu de Nuict, 1985).

22. Homer, *The Iliad, XIII–XXIV*, trans. John Wesley (London: Macmillan, 1902); Homer, *Odyssey*, trans. Stanley Lombardo (Indianapolis: Hackett Publishing Company, 2000), 74.

23. Émile Benveniste, "Expression indo-européenne de l'éternité," *Bulletin de la Societé de linguistique française* 38 (1937): 103–112; Richard Broxton Onians, *The Origins of European Thought* (Cambridge: Cambridge University Press, 1951), 244; Enzo Degani, *Aión da Omero ad Aristotele* (Padua: Cedam, 1961); Éric Alliez, "Aion," in *Vocabulaire européen des philosophies* (Paris: Seuil, 2004), 44–46.

24. Plotinus, *Enneads* III, 7, 11, 44.

25. Boethius, *The Consolation of Philosophy*, ed. and trans. Joel C. Relihan (Indianapolis: Hackett, 2001), 145.

26. Jorge Luis Borges, *Selected Non-fictions*, ed. Eliot Weinberger, trans. Esther Allen and Suzanne Jill Levine (New York: Viking, 1999), 1:136.

27. Borges, *Other Inquisitions, 1937–1952*, trans. Ruth L. C. Simms (Austin: University of Texas, 1964), 180.

28. Plotinus, *Enneads* III, 7, 2.

29. Plotinus, *Enneads* III, 7, 3; see also Federica Montevecchi, *Giorgio Colli: biografia intellettuale* (Turin: Bollati Boringhieri, 2004).

30. Roberto Diodato, *Vermeer, Góngora, Spinoza: l'estetica come scienza intuitiva* (Milan: Mondadori, 1997); on Spinoza's cultural environment, see Steven Nadler, *Spinoza: A Life* (Cambridge: Cambridge University Press, 1999).

31. For a discussion of Rembrandt's self-portraits, see Josua Bruyn et al., *Stitching Foundation Rembrandt Research Project: A Corpus of Rembrandt Paintings*, vol. 4: *Self-Portraits*, trans. D. Cook-Radmore (Dordrecht: Springer, 2005); H. Perry Chapman, *Rembrandt's Self-Portraits: A Study in Seventeenth-Century Identity* (Princeton, N.J.: Princeton University Press, 1990); Flavio Caroli, *L'anima e il volto: ritratto e fisiognomia da Leonardo a Bacon* (Milan: Electa, 1998); Arthur K. Wheelock Jr., "Rembrandt's Self-Portraits: The Creation of a Myth," in *Rembrandt, Rubens, and the Art of Their Time: Recent Perspectives. Papers in Art History from the Pennsylvania State University*, ed. Roland E. Fleisher and Susan C. Scott (University Park: Pennsylvania State University, 1997), 11:12–36; Francesco Bianco, "Pittura come autobiografia: il caso Rembrandt," in *Colloquium philosophicum: Annali del Dipartimento di Filosofia dell'Università degli studi di Roma* V–VI (1998–1999, 1999–2000): 43–63.

32. Julius Langbehn, *Rembrandt als Erzieher* (Weimar: A. Dunker, 1922).

33. Georg Simmel, *Rembrandt: An Essay in the Philosophy of Art*, ed. and trans. Alan Scott and Helmut Staubmann (New York: Routledge, 2005), 6.

34. Ibid., 74.

35. Regarding this antithesis between Italian and German art, a contraposition that Simmel took up in his debate with Burckhardt and that was later developed by Wölfflin, see Jacob Burckhardt, "Rembrandt," in *Werke: Kritische Gesamtausgabe* (Munich-Basel: C.H. Beck-Schwabe & Co., 2003), 13:204–226; and Andrea Pinotti, *Estetica della pittura*, 110.

36. Simmel, *Rembrandt*, 9, 10.

37. See also Franco Rella, *Negli occhi di Vincent: l'io nello specchio del mondo* (Milan: Feltrinelli, 1988), 52–67.

38. Simon Schama, *Rembrandt's Eyes* (New York: Knopf, 1999), 13.

39. Georg Simmel, *The View of Life: Four Metaphysical Essays*, trans. John A. Y. Andrews and Donald N. Levine (Chicago: University of Chicago Press, 2010), 11–12.

40. G. W. F. Hegel, *The Phenomenology of Spirit (The Phenomenology of Mind)*, trans. J. B. Baillie (Lawrence, Kan.: Digireads.com, 2009), 49–50.

41. Simmel, *Rembrandt*, 49.

42. Gottfried Keller, *Ursula*, trans. Bayard Quincy Morgan (New York: Mondial, 2008), 18.

43. Ibid., 18.

44. Paul Celan, *Selections*, ed. Pierre Joris (Berkeley: University of California Press, 2005), 149ff.

45. Benedictus de Spinoza, *Complete Works*, ed. Samuel Shirley and Michael Morgan (Indianapolis: Hackett, 2002), 250.

46. Benedictus de Spinoza, *Ethics*, ed. and trans. G. H. R. Parkinson (Oxford: Oxford University Press, 2000), Part 5, Proposition 24.

47. Ibid., Part 3, Preface.

48. Ibid., Part 4, Proposition 67.

49. Ibid., Part 5, Proposition 23; for a different point of view, see Gilles Deleuze, *Spinoza: immortalité et éternité* (Paris: Gallimard, 2002).

50. Ernst Bloch, *The Spirit of Utopia*, trans. Anthony A. Nassar (Stanford, Calif.: Stanford University Press, 2000), 9.

51. Diogenes Laertius, *The Lives and Opinions of Eminent Philosophers*, VI, 21 (London: H. G. Bohn, 1853), 189.

52. Heraclitus, *Fragments*, trans. and ed. T. M. Robinson (Toronto: University of Toronto Press, 1991), 33 (Fragment 45).

COMMONALITIES

TIMOTHY C. CAMPBELL, SERIES EDITOR

Roberto Esposito, *Terms of the Political: Community, Immunity, Biopolitics*. Translated by Rhiannon Noel Welch. Introduction by Vanessa Lemm.

Maurizio Ferraris, *Documentality: Why It Is Necessary to Leave Traces*. Translated by Richard Davies.

Dimitris Vardoulakis, *Sovereignty and Its Other: Toward the Dejustification of Violence*.

Anne Emmanuelle Berger, *The Queer Turn in Feminism: Identities, Sexualities, and the Theater of Gender*. Translated by Catherine Porter.

James D. Lilley, *Common Things: Romance and the Aesthetics of Belonging in Atlantic Modernity*.

Jean-Luc Nancy, *Identity: Fragments, Frankness*. Translated by François Raffoul.

Miguel Vatter, *Between Form and Event: Machiavelli's Theory of Political Freedom*.

Miguel Vatter, *The Republic of the Living: Biopolitics and the Critique of Civil Society*.

Maurizio Ferraris, *Where Are You? An Ontology of the Cell Phone*. Translated by Sarah De Sanctis.

Irving Goh, *The Reject: Community, Politics, and Religion after the Subject*.

Kevin Attell, *Giorgio Agamben: Beyond the Threshold of Deconstruction*.

J. Hillis Miller, *Communities in Fiction*.

Remo Bodei, *The Life of Things, the Love of Things*. Translated by Murtha Baca.

Gabriela Basterra, *The Subject of Freedom: Kant, Levinas*.

Roberto Esposito, *Categories of the Impolitical*. Translated by Connal Parsley.